"Just say the Word…"

Faith Food From The
Words & Works
Of

Jesus

By Minoli Haththotuwa

Foreword

Y ou have in your hands a short book that has the
power to transform your life. This book con-
tains some of the Scriptures and inspired messages
from Minoli Haththotuwa's global internet ministry.
Testimonies of the transforming Word of the Lord
between these covers have already been recorded
and can be found on her web site www.wingslikeea-
gles.info. Each chapter in this book has the power to
change the way you see, the way you hear and the
life you lead. What you do with the revealed truths
depends upon you, so choose wisely.

Minoli Haththotuwa is an example of how these
truths can transform a life. Her writing comes from
real life experiences and encounters with God. I
encourage you to take each chapter and read it several times. Read it out loud. Read parts of it as dec-
larations over your life. Just say the Word and move
into a deeper and more intimate relationship with the
Lord so that you can let your light shine in the darkness and fulfill your potential in God the Father who
loves you with an everlasting love, and has demon-

strated this love in every way through His son Jesus
Christ.

David Ruleman
Director, Region 11
International Association of Healing Rooms
www.healingroomsregion11.com
June 2010

Introduction

"Just Say The Word" is a collection of individual messages which are intended to encourage and inspire the reader. It is chicken soup for the spirit! The messages focus on some of the things the Lord Jesus said and did. They remind us that in the name of Jesus and the power of His Spirit we have the authority to speak the words He spoke and do the works He did. The messages in this book were originally written as weekly 'eWords' for the website www.wingslikeeagles.info. Each stand-alone chapter consists of a passage of Scripture and its application. It would make a good travelling companion, a motivating devotional, or a useful group study guide. Reading this book will feed your faith and stir your heart to take Jesus seriously. The messages are all a result of time spent soaking in God's presence and receiving a strength and joy which made me feel like I could climb the highest mountain! Jesus said: *"I tell you the truth, anyone who has faith in me will do what I have been doing. He will do even greater things than these, because I am going to the Father"*

– *John 14:12*. All things are possible to those who believe! Power and strength to you in the mighty name of Jesus!

Minoli Haththotuwa

Dedication

This book is dedicated to the One whose name makes all things possible – the Lord Jesus Christ, the Son of God and the Savior of the world. He transformed my life and gave me a new song in my heart!

I thank God for the loving support of my family, in all the assignments I step into. I also remember the men and women of God who have impacted my life and stirred in me a hunger for the Word and a heart to delve into it, especially Dr Tissa Weerasingha, of Calvary Church, Sri Lanka, who was our mentor and pastor for many years.

Contents

"The centurion replied, 'Lord, I do not deserve to have you come under my roof. But just say the word, and my servant will be healed'."
Matthew 8:8

Chapter One

Faith To See
(Matthew 9:27-31)

"As Jesus went on from there, two blind men followed Him, calling out, "Have mercy on us, Son of David!" When He had gone indoors, the blind men came to Him, and He asked them, "Do you believe that I am able to do this?" "Yes Lord," they replied. Then He touched their eyes and said, "According to your faith will it be done to you"; and their sight was restored. Jesus warned them sternly, "See that no one knows about this." But they went out and spread the news about Him all over that region."

This message carries a simple key which can open locked doors - **faith!**

Blindness is an affliction that seems to have occurred frequently in Bible times, and the Bible speaks of several types. One was the result of old age, as with Isaac (Genesis 27:1) and Eli (1 Samuel

3:2). Blindness was also seen as a curse or punishment, and a divine act, as in the case of the men of Sodom (Genesis 19:11), the Syrian army (2 Kings 6:18) and Elymas the sorcerer (Acts 13:11). From John 9:2 we see that people also sometimes regarded blindness as a result of generational sin.

People of the day believed that blindness was something permanent which could only be healed through divine intervention. A man Jesus healed of blindness said (John 9:32 & 33) *"Nobody has ever heard of opening the eyes of a man born blind. If this man were not from God, he could do nothing."* We see many such instances where Jesus did what people perceived as impossible, and healed the blind. The recovery of sight to the blind was a part of His mission on earth (Isaiah 61:1). He opened both physical and spiritual eyes as He brought people to salvation and a revelation of the love of God.

In this passage of Scripture, the Lord Jesus had been travelling through many places, teaching and preaching, with signs and wonders following Him. Just before He met these blind men, He had freed two people from humanly irreversible situations. (He had brought a dead girl to life, and healed a woman who had been sick with an 'incurable' disease for 12 years).

As Jesus travelled to His next destination, these blind men followed Him, calling out to Him and crying out for mercy. These men had probably heard of the miracles that followed Jesus wherever He went. Society had relegated them to a life in the dark, and they had no reason to hope that things could ever be different. All they had been capable of doing was to sit by the road and beg. Their daily sustenance had been dependent on the unreliable mercy of man, as days passed in a world of darkness and frustration they had been helpless to change. They had been in a prison from which there was no escape. They had hitherto believed they could have no control over their destiny, but there is nothing impossible with God! Hope arose in their hearts, as they began to hear stories of Jesus and how He healed and delivered. Whoever encountered Him was radically touched and made whole. The ones who sat in darkness began to see a flicker of light! Jesus was heading for their town. Was it possible that their eyes could be opened? Was there a chance that they would be able to see?

The first step towards radical healing and restoration is to see the possibility of change and desire it. We will never attempt to change what we tolerate. We have to want change badly enough to decide to step out of a dead-end situation and reach out for something better. Many of us live with a level of sickness, oppression, disturbed sleep, abuse from those close to us, and frequent financial losses, when God wants us to see another level of living (in His abundance and blessing) and long for radical change! John 10:10 tells us that the thief comes only to steal, kill and destroy, but Jesus came that we may have life and have it to the full. Why should we settle for anything less than the best He wants to give us?

It is hard to imagine how two blind people followed the Lord Jesus as He moved through crowded streets. They probably held on to each other, and to some kind person who led them along. There must have been crowds thronging around Him; people following Him and asking to touch Him and be touched, as they felt the power and anointing flowing from Him, and longed for it to impact their lives. We can imagine the desperate, sick, demon-bound people who ran after Jesus, pushing through the crowds, the stronger getting ahead of the weak.

It was a rough road for these men who could not see. For them, each step forward was one they had to take in faith, trusting someone else, or trusting their senses of hearing and touch. But hope kept them going forward, a step at a time.

Faith and expectation are the perfect grounds for a miracle. If faith is being sure of what we hope for and certain of what we do not see (Hebrews 11:1), these men were the ideal candidates for a miracle. They believed in the power of someone they could not physically see. What had been a situation of long term darkness was suddenly opening to the light of resurrection life, and **it all began with someone considering a possibility**. These men could not see Jesus with their physical eyes but with each step they took towards Him, He became more real to them until they began to see Him in their hearts. They were so desperate for His touch that they kept calling His name and crying out to Him as they stumbled over the uneven, stony roads. Perhaps they knocked into people and things, and hurt themselves as they went along, but they were on a mission, and not to be hindered. They called Him 'Son of David'. This was an acknowledgement of His Lordship and Kingship, and His sovereign power. ('Son of David' was a popular Jewish title for the Messiah and King prophesied from ages past). They were calling on the Savior to touch them and free them from a life of darkness; they were crying out for His eternal mercy and forgiveness, as they longed to live in the glory of His light. They were not deterred by anything or anyone - they kept crying out to Jesus!

When these two men finally stood before Jesus, they heard Him ask them *"Do you believe that I am able to do this?"* This probably made their faith even stronger. Jesus knew their need! They believed! Their faith was already high, because they had followed Jesus through the streets, and all they had heard were the praises to God, and the joy of those He touched and healed as He passed along the way. As they stood before Jesus, they were still in darkness; but they could feel the waves of anointing, the awesome power, and the sweet holiness of His Person! They could hear the authority in His voice, and feel His love, as He spoke to them, and sought their hearts.

These men had no doubt that God was here to set them free! As Jesus touched their eyes, He said *"According to your faith will it be done to you"*. They both received an instant miracle as tissues were recreated, muscles and optic nerves came alive, and the eyes that had never seen were made new by the breath of God! It was a creative miracle! It was a new birth. It was an unforgettable awakening for these men, when their eyes were opened and the first sight they ever saw was the love in the eyes of Jesus! They were looking into the eyes of eternity. It was a time-less, 'forever' moment. It is possible to imagine that they were unable to look away from the light on His face, or do anything but fall at His feet and worship Him, their King and Lord, the Son of David! Here was glory. Here was Healing Love. They received total healing as Jesus touched them and their eyes were opened, spiritual as well as physical. The painful scars of years of rejection, emptiness, and isolation were washed away in those moments of being held in the presence of radical atoning love. If their blind-ness had been perceived in the community as a result of sin, they had probably lived under a spirit of false guilt and condemnation all their lives. Now they felt forgiven and clean. The burden was lifted! It was the start of a new life for them both. No more labels; no more limitations; no more darkness. They were free!

Friend, you may be someone who has had to endure a difficult and painful situation for a long time. Maybe you have got tired of praying for a change. Maybe you have told yourself that God will heal you or change your situation if He wants to. Perhaps you believe that what you face is a part of God's will for you; or maybe you have got so accustomed to toler-ating your pain that you have adjusted your life to accommodate it.

The Lord Jesus is looking at your heart today in the light of His Word. He is asking you the question He asked the two men who were longing to break out from the darkness and see. *"Do you believe that I am able to do this?"* Or has the intensity and persistence of your problem blinded you to the greatness of Almighty God, and the fact that there is nothing too hard for Him? You may have started to believe that your situation can never change, and that you will have to live with it till the end of your life. This is not true. The devil is a liar, and has been trying to come between God and man from the dawn of time! He brings these hopeless thoughts, and anti-God reasoning into our minds because He wants to destroy our faith, and our relationship with our Heavenly Father.

There would have been people who tried to stop the two blind men from going to Jesus. They may have been stronger people with perfect vision who pushed them aside as they forged ahead to touch the Master. Perhaps Jesus did not even hear them when they first began to call on His name. But they kept on calling; they kept on following! Nothing deterred them. They believed He was the answer to their lifelong bondage! They knew that they had everything to gain if they could only reach His side.

Their perseverance paid off! We too need to persevere and not give up. We need to keep calling on the name of the Lord, no matter what; to keep following Him and seeking Him as He has asked us to do: *"Call to Me and I will answer you..."* (Jeremiah 33:3). *"Ask and it will be given unto you"* (Matthew 7:7).

Maybe you have let go of hope, and have stopped believing for a miracle in your life. When in our humanity we cannot seem to do what the Word tells us to do, we can always ask the Holy Spirit to teach us how to. If you have lost your faith and settled for less than God's best, you could ask Him to teach you true faith. He is able to help you to believe again for the impossible! Begin to feed your spirit with the Word of God, and the testimonies of others, and see your faith grow! You will experience the Holy Spirit teaching you, and lifting your expectations to a whole new height. There will come a moment when nothing will seem impossible or difficult for you, in the Lord Jesus Christ. Then Jesus can say *"According to your faith will it be done to you"*, and you will see mountains move and the most amazing miracles breaking forth in your life and ministry. **In the system of the world we have to see to believe; in the Kingdom of God, we have to believe to see.** *"So we fix our eyes not on what is seen, but on what is unseen. For what is seen is temporary, but what is unseen is eternal."* (2 Corinthians 4:18).

The two men who came to Jesus believed before they saw, and they saw because they believed! They received such a radical miracle in their lives because:

- They decided to seek change (however impossible it seemed).
- They knew it had to be through Jesus.
- They were desperate for Jesus – they kept calling His name and seeking Him undeterred.
- They acknowledged that Jesus was Messiah and Lord.

- They believed that He had the power to make it happen – they had faith.

I pray that you will say 'yes' to change today, and begin to believe again that nothing is impossible with God - for yourself, for those you love, for your church, community and nation. There is no situation our God cannot turn around. Like the man in Mark 9:24, who needed a miracle, maybe we need to say *"I do believe; but help me overcome my unbelief"*! God's power is activated when we believe. He is pleased when He sees our faith (Hebrews 11:6) and knows we trust Him against all odds. Not many of us would be inclined to help a person who did not really believe we could get the job done!

Know that the One who is in you is greater than the one in the world (1 John 4:4) and He will enable you to believe! He is King of kings and Lord of lords; the Name above every name. He is Jesus. He is Power. He wants to heal and prosper you! May every darkening doubt be banished, in the name of Jesus, and may you believe for the impossible, and see it come to pass. May you call on the name of Jesus, and seek after Him with all your heart. May you receive His touch now! *"Arise, shine, for your light has come…"!* (Isaiah 60:1).

Notes:

Chapter Two

The Way (John 14:1-6)

"Do not let your hearts be troubled. Trust in God; trust also in me. In my Father's house are many rooms; if it were not so, I would have told you. I am going there to prepare a place for you. And if I go and prepare a place for you, I will come back and take you to be with me that you also may be where I am. You know the way to the place where I am going."

Thomas said to Him, "Lord, we don't know where you are going, so how can we know the way?" Jesus answered, "I am the way and the truth and the life. No one comes to the Father except through me."

Jesus spoke these words to His disciples shortly before His crucifixion. His disciples had walked and talked with Him for three years. They had been blessed daily by the anointing and strength of His presence. They constantly received an impartation of power and love in every word He spoke and each touch of His hand. Now He was telling them that He would be leaving them, and it was too much for them to bear – they were anxious, fearful and confused. They could not imagine a life without the power of the presence of Jesus!

This message is about how Jesus reassured His disciples that although He was going away, it was really to take them to something better. This message is God's assurance to each of His precious sons and daughters, that although you may be facing rough times right now, He is taking you to something far better!

The stages in the Jewish betrothal and marriage rites are the background for what Jesus was saying to His disciples when He told them He was going away to prepare a place for them. In the days of Jesus, a betrothal would begin when the prospective bridegroom would visit the home of the prospective bride and offer her the terms of their contract of marriage (mainly the duties expected of a wife). If she was agreeable to his terms, they would seal their betrothal in the presence of the father of the bride-to-be by drinking from the same cup of wine. Then the young man would depart to his father's house, and work on building or renovating a separate room for his bride. This could typically take many months. When the new room was ready, he would return to take the young lady back home as his wife, at a time and day appointed by his father.

This is what the Lord was telling his friends – that he was going away, but only to make ready a special place for them in His Father's house! He was going to take them to all the heavenly blessing that was prepared for them. They were dismayed and heavy-hearted, but Jesus was only going so that they could move up into a higher level. They had depended on Him thus far, and walked in a certain level of anointing, but after His departure, they would receive the Holy Spirit and be mighty men of Power. Jesus said to them (John 14:12) *"I tell you the truth, anyone who has faith in me will do what I have been doing. He will do even greater things than these, because I am going to the Father."*

There is so much that God Infinite has for you and me, and we have not even begun to scratch the surface! In the Father's house are many rooms! There is so much revelation, love, anointing, power, holiness, provision, healing, wisdom, gifts, in the Father's house - more than we have ever asked for or imagined! He has more for us than we will ever be able to fully explore.

The Lord Jesus bought us the ultimate victory upon the cross and gave us the power of His name. He drank from the cup of His suffering, and gave it to us to drink. He made it possible for us to be partakers, and partners in His sacrifice. He sealed our betrothal with His sinless blood. Then He went away to prepare the way for His children to move in the power of the Spirit. He made it possible for us to step up into a higher level of dominion and authority, and walk in the same power that raised Him from the grave. We are kings and priests – the offspring of the Most High God, and joint heirs with Jesus Christ. Some of us are struggling or defeated in aspects of our lives, when Jesus already prepared a place for us to rule and reign! He wants to take us to that higher ground. He wants us to take hold of the power and authority He has already vested in us, that we may walk in victory, in joy, and in the fullness of the abundant life that He came to give. Yes, there are many hindrances along the way, and the enemy constantly tries to block us from the blessing of God. But what did the Lord tell His disciples?

1) Do not let your hearts be troubled – We spend too much time in anxiety, worrying and fearful about the future, or manipulating our circumstances so that we can get out of the difficult situations we are in right now. Believe the truth that Jesus has already prepared a place for you! He has already released the solution you seek. Ephesians 1:3 says *"Praise be to the God and Father of our Lord Jesus Christ, who has blessed us in the heavenly realms with every spiritual blessing in Christ."* God has already credited our spiritual account with every good thing we could ever need! However, if we continue to give in to the fear the enemy brings and anticipate the worst, then we block our own blessing and will never see the goodness God has for us.

2) Trust in God; trust also in me – This is faith! Receive God's Word; believe it, speak it, sing it, think it. Walk in the power of His promises and see them fulfilled. Faith can only grow when we feed on the Word of God and live in the expectation of its reality in our daily lives. God said to the people of Israel

(Deuteronomy 6:6) *"These commandments that I give you today are to be upon your hearts. Impress them on your children. Talk about them when you sit at home and when you walk along the road, when you lie down and when you get up. Tie them as symbols on your hands and bind them on your foreheads. Write them on the door frames of your houses and on your gates."* This may sound extreme but it is God's prescription for walking in faith. Unless the Word saturates us, it is not possible to develop the faith it takes to see the power of God manifested in every aspect of our lives.

3) Follow 'the Way' - Jesus said *"I am the Way, the Truth and the Life"*. He was and is the only way. He told the disciples (John 3:34) *"A new command I give you: Love one another. By this all men will know that you are my disciples, if you love one another."* He is God; God is love; Thomas said to Jesus *"we don't know the way to where you are going"* but He had already shown them the way – it was Jesus; it was Love. There is no other way to the blessings of heaven but to fix our eyes on our Savior and to walk the **'Jesus'** way – in **faith** and in **love**. It is so simple and still so difficult, but that is why the Holy Spirit came, to help us to walk a heavenly road on earth; to step upwards daily into the glorious blessings that Jesus has prepared for us to know. *"I have come that they may have life and have it to the full."* (John 10:10) This is God's provision for you!

My prayer is that you will make a conscious decision today, to refuse to allow fear and anxiety into your hearts. *"Do not let your hearts be troubled"*, but meditate on the Word and choose to trust God instead. Choose to walk in 'the way', and see the glorious things that have been prepared for you in the Father's House! Jesus is taking you to the greater things He has in store for you.

Notes:

Chapter Three

New Wineskins
(Luke 5:33-39)

"They said to Him, "John's disciples often fast and pray, and so do the disciples of the Pharisees, but yours go on eating and drinking." Jesus answered, "Can you make the guests of the bridegroom fast while He is with them? But the time will come when the bridegroom will be taken from them; in those days they will fast." He told them this parable: "No one tears a patch from a new garment and sews it on an old one. If he does, he will have torn the new garment, and the patch from the new will not match the old. And no one pours new wine into old wineskins. If he does, the new wine will burst the skins, the wine will run out, and the wineskins will be ruined. No, new wine must be poured into new wineskins. And no one after drinking old wine wants the new for he says the old is better."

People who watched Jesus were confused. They could not seem to figure Him out! He was a spiritual leader, and a man (as they saw Him) in touch with the supernatural; a man who did great miracles, signs and wonders, but somehow, he did not seem to fit the stereotype. He did not fit the image people had for a minister of God. He laughed and cried, He enjoyed life, He ate and drank, He wore what He wanted and went where He was led. He was so **free!** Who was He? Why was He not like them? The religious spirits around him were perplexed. They pondered about Him until they could bear it no more, and finally asked Him why He was so different! They asked Jesus why He and His disciples were not fasting and praying all day; in their book, the men of God were supposed to be controlled, quiet and sober, and meditating on the Scriptures, with fasting and prayer. They were supposed to act the part! Jesus answered the people that a time for fasting and intense prayer was coming, but until then it was a season of feasting and holy rejoicing – the Bridegroom was with His guests! They were to make the most of His presence - to absorb His love and His power, and to learn from Him. Further down the line, when the church was born and persecution began, they would have to fast and pray.

Most people are only happy with what they can comfortably slot into different shaped boxes. Our Lord refused to be boxed in. He refused to be limited. There is always pressure, even in our life in Christ, to allow ourselves to be boxed in, just to receive the acceptance and acknowledgement of those around us.

This is a danger we always face. When we step into the boundaries of human expectation and opinion, we immediately limit what God wants to do in and through our lives. We deny ourselves so much of the real power and blessing of God because we get into a man made box, and stop seeing beyond it. When we do this, we submit to the religious spirits so active in the world (and even in the church), whose mission is to stop the free flow of the Holy Spirit among people, and hinder the Kingdom of God. We subject ourselves to fleshly control, which also hinders personal spiritual growth, and the revelation and power we can live in. It causes us to place greater importance on the views of man rather than upon the will of God.

Jesus told the people that a piece of new cloth could not be used as a patch on an old garment - they can never become one. This is because the patch of new cloth would shrink when washed and the whole garment would be ruined. In the same way, He said that new wine could not be poured into old wineskins, lest the wineskin burst and the wine be wasted. In Jesus' day, wine was stored in wineskins. New wine had to be stored in a new wineskin because the new wineskin would stretch to fit fermenting new wine. An older wineskin would be hard and dry (because it had already stretched to its limit and lost its flexibility) and would eventually burst because it could not stretch to accommodate the fermenting new wine.

What did Jesus mean here? He was talking about what the 'born again' life really should be. In the Book of John chapter 3, Jesus said to Nicodemus *"flesh gives birth to flesh, but the Spirit gives birth to spirit.*

You should not be surprised at my saying, 'You must be born again'. The wind blows wherever it pleases. You hear its sound, but you cannot tell where it comes from or where it is going. So it is with everyone born of the Spirit...." Jesus was saying that once we are born again and filled with the Holy Spirit, we cannot continue to live in the old way, or have some aspects of our old fleshly life still prevailing. We cannot sew a patch of 'new life' (the life in the Spirit) upon our old beliefs and values. Everything had to be radically new! He was saying that we have to become completely transformed new wineskins, temples of the Holy Spirit, filled with the new wine - the presence, power and love of the Holy Spirit. Jesus meant that we cannot be born again and continue to exist on the carnal realm which was our portion in the past - there is better, and bigger, and more beautiful for us now – a complete overhaul! New wine needs new wineskins! Attempting to walk in the Spirit while still thinking and feeling in the flesh can be disastrous. This could make the wineskin 'burst', leading to manifestations of chronic sicknesses, mental depression, or emotional pain and confusion; it is not possible to have one foot in the Spirit, and one foot in the world, and walk in victory.

This is sad, but true of many who believe they are disciples of the Lord Jesus Christ, but live on a shallow level of dual identity which grieves the heart of God. Sadder still is what Jesus said - that some people actually prefer the 'old wine'. The old wine stands for ritual, tradition, religion, and the works that we tried to do to win brownie points with God, before we came into this love relationship which draws us into His arms from day to day. The old wine is the panacea of the majority. It is like a drug, which satisfies the flesh. The old wine can be measured and controlled, and it can be manipulated by the pourer, to create an appearance of holiness and dedication to God. This is safe; this is familiar. But the new Holy Spirit wine is exciting, dizzy, and powerful. When the new wine is poured out, the Pourer (God) does what He wills (John 3:8 - *'The wind blows wherever it pleases'*). He releases a spirit of worship which brings down God's presence and power, and the joy of the Lord. Who knows what the Spirit will do when He is given freedom to flow as He wills!

God wants us to be new wineskins filled with new wine! He wants our bodies to be holy temples of the Holy Spirit (1 Corinthians 6:19), and our minds to be transformed and renewed by the Word of God (Romans 12:2). Open your heart to God today. Come before Him in worship and surrender your **'all'** to Him. He wants to fill you with His Spirit, with effervescent, joyful new wine. His heart desires that we break out of every human box, mental and spiritual, and allow Him the freedom to work and flow into and through our lives. His new wine is an overflowing river, filled with beautiful blessing and benefit, which like real new wine continues to bubble, ferment, and increase as it is received to fill every part of the new wineskin. It is a freedom from bondage, contagious joy, healing, and favor wherever we turn!

It could be that you need God's radical touch upon your life because you have never been truly free. Give your wineskin wholly to Jesus today. As Paul wrote to the Romans in chapter 12:1 *"Therefore I urge you, brothers, in view of God's mercy, to offer your bodies as living sacrifices, holy and pleasing to God - this is your spiritual act of worship...."* In this act of worship, as we surrender ourselves to God and to a life of holiness and purity from day to day, the New Wine begins to seep in little by little, until the temple is wholly consecrated to the Almighty. The devil cannot touch what is marked by the Lord and dedicated unto Him!

As we receive the infilling of the New Wine, we move towards the life God calls us to – a life of radical love and power; a life of radical victory and miracles, signs and wonders. He is calling us to sweet and deep communion with Him (Deep calling to deep), where in the secret places of the Most High, the wineskin is daily filled with New Wine. New Wine brings the enabling to break free of every human limitation, benchmark and religious tradition, to live a life of New Testament purpose - for the glory of the King of kings and the Lord of lords! Our Lord is coming back and the days are drawing nearer. We cannot sit on the fence - we have to walk in the passion and purpose of the King!

May your wineskin be filled with New Wine. May the radical power and presence of our radical Almighty God transform your life, in Jesus' name, Amen!

Notes:

Chapter Four

The Better Thing (Luke 10:38-42)

"As Jesus and His disciples were on their way, He came to a village where a woman named Martha opened her home to Him. She had a sister called Mary, who sat at the Lord's feet listening to what He said. But Martha was distracted by all the preparations that had to be made. She came to Him and asked, "Lord, don't you care that my sister has left me to do the work by myself? Tell her to help me!" "Martha, Martha" the Lord answered, "you are worried and upset about many things, but only one thing is needed. Mary has chosen what is better, and it will not be taken away from her."

This passage of Scripture is about how Jesus and His disciples visited Martha's home, which was in Bethany, near Jerusalem. Jesus loved this family and frequently visited their home (John 11:5). Martha was probably a widow and the owner of the house. Jesus was rejected by many of the Jews and religious leaders, who refused to accept His claims or receive His words, and although it may have been dangerous to entertain Him, Martha welcomed Him with open arms.

Picture the scenario: Jesus, entered the home, was greeted warmly, and sat down to rest from his travels. From the moment He walked in, Mary was drawn to Him. She was drawn to the anointing which compelled her closer, until she stationed herself at His feet. She felt the power of each word He spoke; she watched Him mesmerized, as words flowed from His heart, into hers, because the words of Jesus are life and Spirit. (John 6:63: *"The words I have spoken to you are spirit and they are life."*) And *"The testimony of Jesus is the spirit of prophecy"* (Revelations 19:10). Mary sat at the Master's feet. She did not ask Him for anything, or tell Him any of her problems and concerns. Her heart was open; she was listening to every word He spoke. She was absorbing His love and powerful presence.

Martha on the other hand was the typical hostess. What she was doing was very good and needful; she knew the Lord needed food and drink, and she was probably under pressure because Jesus was an unexpected guest, and she still wanted to 'put on a good show' and give Him the best she had. She did not have a freezer from which she could whip out some pre-made delicacy and pop into the microwave! It is possible to picture her rushing around, hot and bothered, baking bread, maybe slaughtering a goat or lamb, cooking, serving, etc, and too busy to really focus on Jesus or anything He said. The Word of God tells us she was distracted by all the preparations she had to make. She could have made her honored guest feel very uncomfortable and concerned that His presence was an inconvenience - she went so far as to accuse Jesus of not caring about all the work she had to do, and to complain that her sister was not helping her! She was voluntarily making an elaborate meal to impress her guests, but feeling sorry for herself at the same time. She was probably thinking (as some of us may have!) 'poor me, no one ever helps me'; and 'I have to do all the work around here'! She was not really serving the Lord at all...

There are a few things we can learn from Martha:

1) **She took a burden upon herself which was not hers to take.** She really had no right to grumble to the Lord! Jesus said in Matthew 11:30 *"For my yoke is easy and my burden is light."* God always sustains us to do the things He has called us to do.

2) She was resentful that her sister sat at the feet of Jesus and soaked in the anointed Word. It is true that there was work to do, but **it was all about the choice she made.** Life can be frantically busy, but we have to make the right choices (however difficult) as we prioritize how we spend our time. If this means we have to make a trade off, even a costly one - so be it. There is no gain without pain! Those

costly offerings are the true sacrifices which are pleasing to the Lord.

3) It is true that Jesus and His disciples needed food and it is commendable that Martha was meeting their need; but she was exhausting herself to make an impression. **She was on a futile treadmill of people pleasing.** We may have all been in this place, but it is an empty work of the flesh. The world tells us that 'more is better', and 'big is beautiful' (!) so even in Christian ministry, we rush around trying to get 'more' done, but our works (and the number of them) are not what God is looking for. He is more concerned with seeing the heart quality of what we bring to Him. He then brings forth the quantity! He brings a natural multiplication to what is done through His leading and in the right spirit.

4) **It is all about the attitude.** Our service is not a fragrant offering to God if done resentfully or grudgingly. The offering God receives as precious incense and a pleasing sacrifice of worship is the heart of love and joy with which we bring it.

We can learn the better thing from Mary:

1) **She made the right choice.** She listened to her heart. Her reasoning probably told her she needed to help Martha with the preparation of the meal, but her heart drew her to the eyes, voice, and presence of Jesus, as she was

riveted to His feet and drank in the power of each life giving word He spoke.

2) **She stayed at the feet of Jesus.** There are always a million distractions to take us away from God's presence, even once we have decided to come away and get alone with Him, including the many thoughts and 'reminders' which suddenly seem to pop up in our minds as we seek to focus on the Lord. Martha was grumbling and resentful towards Mary and in addition to her words, she probably sighed, flashed some strong looks at Mary, and bustled around noisily to make her feel guilty, and prompt her to get up and help! But Mary stayed where she was. If you can see your time alone with Jesus as something necessary for your survival and growth, you would never feel guilty about getting away to be alone with Him, whatever anyone says or does, or whatever distracting thoughts the enemy throws at you!

3) **Mary knew how to listen.** We spend too much time talking to God and telling Him what He should be doing for us! If we could simply learn to make our hearts quiet before Him and listen, we would hear what He has to say, and the answers and direction we need to every pressing problem we face.

4) **Mary humbled herself – she sat at Jesus' feet.** It was a time for her to receive, as she sat on the floor at the feet of Jesus, acknowledging His authority and His Lordship over

her life. Her heart was submitted to His Word. Some of us may be good at pouring out the Word of God, and the gifts that flow with it, but not so good at receiving the same for ourselves. It takes humility to receive!

5) **If we hunger and thirst for righteousness, we will be filled** (Matthew 5:6). If we draw near to God He will draw near to us (James 4:8). If we seek to dwell in the secret places of the Most High, we will surely get to rest in the shadow of the Almighty (Psalm 91:1). Jesus said to Martha that Mary had made the right choice and it would not be taken away from her. Mary was hungry for the presence of Jesus. If we truly seek the presence of God and sincerely long to stay at His feet, and be held close to His heart, God will make it possible for us in terms of time and space, regardless of our schedules. It is all about choosing the better thing!

Friend, in this end time hour, there is nothing more important than seeking and soaking in the presence of God. Everything we need is found in His presence - not only healing and provision, but protection from the constant battle that rages against us, revelation and wisdom from the Word, the anointing and fragrance of Jesus on our lives, the power to do great exploits for the glory of His name, and the ability to discern the times and seasons. I pray that you will choose to do the better thing because *"the Spirit and the Bride say 'Come!' And let him who hears say, 'Come!' Whoever is thirsty, let him come; and whoever wishes, let him take the free gift of the water of life'."* (Revelations 22:17)". He is found by those who seek Him with all their hearts. (Jeremiah 29:13). Be like Mary; choose the better thing!

Notes:

Chapter Five

The Greater Name
(Luke 9:46-48)

"An argument started among the disciples as to which of them would be the greatest. Jesus, knowing their thoughts, took a little child and made him stand beside Him. Then He said to them, "Whoever welcomes this little child in my name welcomes Me; and whoever welcomes Me welcomes the One who sent Me. For he who is least among you all – he is the greatest."

It is quite funny that the disciples were so competitive. They were the closest associates of the Lord Jesus, (supposed to be "super-spiritual" men), and the founders of the church; but like little children, they were arguing about who was better, and who was "greatest", and who would do greater things! Even as they argued, these men must have known that they were being shallow and childish. They probably thought that their conversation was just between the few of them - they knew their argument would not impress the Master. However, Jesus 'saw' their thoughts and dealt with them. They were acting like children, and the Lord took a little child to illustrate a point to them.

The Lord Jesus told His disciples that they were talking through a carnal mindset. The world looks for greatness in terms of educational attainments, experience, maturity, reputation, etc; but what is considered 'greatness' in the world is not what may be acknowledged as 'great' in the Kingdom of God. On the contrary, the Lord demonstrated that greatness is about the reduction of self and the increase of Jesus in our lives and ministries. The world is motivated to greatness through unhealthy comparisons and a spirit of competition, whereas Jesus illustrated that greatness in the Kingdom is about laying down one's life and desires, and surrendering to the will of the greater One. It is about putting the needs of others before one's own.

In the Kingdom, those who humble themselves are exalted (Luke 14:11). The name of Jesus was exalted above every other because He humbled Himself. Philippians 2:6-11 says (about Jesus): *"Who, being in very nature God, did not consider equality with God something to be grasped, but made Himself nothing, taking the very nature of a servant, being made in human likeness, and being found in appearance as a man, He humbled Himself and became obedient to death – even death on a cross! Therefore God exalted Him to the highest place and gave Him the name that is above every name, that at the name of Jesus every knee should bow, in Heaven and on earth and under the earth, and every tongue confess that Jesus Christ is Lord, to the glory of God the Father."*

The only name which is truly 'great' is the name of Jesus, and 'greatness' in our lives is all about His name being glorified. Jesus said *"whoever welcomes this little child in **my name** welcomes Me"*. In other words, our 'greatness' is as much as the extent we lay down our own identity and walk in Jesus and His name. Our 'greatness' is in His name. Whether it is the most senior minister in the largest ministry in the world, or the young Christian who has just been born again, their claim to greatness comes from the name they walk in and how much they allow the name of Jesus to be glorified.

The name of Jesus is higher than every other name. His name stands for power, and might. His name is salvation – it means 'God Saves'. The name of Jesus opens doors – it is the name of the most important person in the universe! It is the name which carries all power and authority over every demonic spirit and every sickness and disease. It is the name above all others, and the one before which every knee shall bow and every tongue confess lordship! (Philippians 2:10 & 11).

Friend, if you could receive a fresh revelation of the power and authority of the name of Jesus, and that you carry all the infinite potential of His name, it could transform your life! When you reach out your hand to pray for someone's healing, it is not you who stretches out a hand, it is Jesus – it is His name which brings the miracle. When you stand firm against the attacks of darkness and resist the devil in the name of Jesus, remember that it is not you who refuses to be moved – it is the Greater One in you. The devil hears the name of Jesus, and trembles and flees (James 4:7). When you stand before the Father's throne and intercede for the need of another in the name of Jesus, it is as though Jesus stands before Him. You are a joint heir with Jesus Christ (Romans 8:17) vested with all the power and authority of His *name*. Jesus said (in Matthew 28:18): *"All authority in heaven and on earth has been given to me."* And Luke 10:19: *"I have given you authority to trample on snakes and scorpions and to overcome all the power of the enemy."* When you come before the Father and pray in Jesus' name, He sees His Son, He hears the **name**! (*"I tell you the truth, my Father will give you whatever you ask **in my name**"* – John 16:23). You are the righteousness of God **in Christ** (2 Corinthians 5:21). You are a chosen and precious child of God – with the blood of Jesus upon your life. You are a carrier of His Name! This is why little children in Africa are ministering healing, and raising the dead – because of the anointing that comes with simple faith in the power of the Name!

Genesis 11:1-9 tells us about the tower of Babel, and how God confused the language of the people building it, and scattered them to different parts of the world. This was because they were building the tower to *'make a name for themselves'* (Genesis 11:4). God will not share His glory with any other (Isaiah 42:8), and the ministry or person seeking to make their own name will ultimately crumble. Jesus used a little child to illustrate His point because children do not have any hidden motives like adults often have. They do not have any desires to promote themselves or make their names "known". He told the disciples that competition, manipulation, promotion and striving were the world's ways to make a name known; His way was the childlike way; faith in a *name!*

Jesus said that whoever welcomes us in His name welcomes Him. To be received in His name, we have to go forth in His name; we have to believe in His name; we have to walk in the power and the authority of His name! This is how even the newest believer can do mighty exploits for Jesus and be 'great' – when we bring honor and glory to His name, and live (in all humility) in the power of that name. John the Baptist said in John 3:30: *"He must become greater; I must become less."* As we make more room for God to be glorified, and allow our own name to be covered by His, this is when His power will truly be seen through our lives. This is the person God regards as 'great'! This is the man or woman Jesus says would be welcomed even as He or the Father would be welcomed, because people begin to see not the finite human 'you', but the power of the name of Almighty God. Jesus said in John 14:23: *"If anyone loves me, he will obey my teaching. My Father will love him, and we will come to him and make our home with him."*

Finally, remember that God loves all His children alike, regardless of who they are or what they do.

Romans 2:11 says *"For God does not show favor-itism"*, while in Acts 10:34-35 Paul wrote *"I now realize how true it is that God does not show favor-itism but accepts men from every nation who fear Him and do what is right."* Whatever we may do to make our name 'great' before God or man, He is only interested in our hearts!

May God reveal afresh to you the power and the reality of the name of Jesus, that you may know true greatness each day – the greatness of the name of Jesus, as His name is exalted and His name alone!

Notes:

Chapter Six

Freed For A Purpose
(Luke 19:28-34)

"After Jesus had said this, He went on ahead, going up to Jerusalem. As He approached Bethphage and Bethany at the hill called the Mount of Olives, He sent two of His disciples, saying to them, "Go to the village ahead of you, and as you enter it, you will find a colt tied there, which no one has ever ridden. Untie it and bring it here. If anyone asks you, "Why are you untying it?" tell him, "The Lord needs it.""

Those who were sent ahead went and found it just as He had told them. As they were untying the colt, its owners asked them, "Why are you untying the colt?" They replied, "The Lord needs it."

This is Luke's account of the Lord Jesus' final journey into Jerusalem before He was crucified. Jesus regularly travelled this road over the Mount of

Olives with His disciples (Luke 22:39). He probably used this route to get to Bethany, to visit His friend Lazarus. This mountain ridge in east Jerusalem (also called Mount Olivet) was named after the olive groves that once covered its slopes. It is mentioned many times in the Gospels as somewhere Jesus went to, when He needed to get alone with God and pray (Luke 19:28-44). It was also a place where He met with His disciples and taught them (Matthew 24), and where He appeared to them after His Resurrection. Jesus also ascended into heaven from the Mount of Olives (Acts 1:1-12). It seems to have been one of His favorite places!

Bethany was about two miles southeast of Jerusalem (John 11:18), and the home of Mary, Martha and Lazarus, while Bethphage was a village near the road from Jericho to Jerusalem. As Jesus and His disciples approached these villages, He instructed two of them to go ahead into the village (probably Bethphage) and bring back a colt which was tied there. They were briefed about how to reply if anyone challenged them when they untied the colt; their answer was simply to be that the Lord needed it!

Imagine how you would feel if you had just bought a beautiful new car and parked it outside your home only to find a stranger getting in behind the wheel and preparing to drive it away! I think we would do a lot more than just ask the culprit what he was doing! However, verses 9-11 of Psalm 50 remind us that everything in the universe belongs to God. He really does not need anything that we could offer Him, but in His own amazing way, He gives us opportunities to receive the abundance of His blessing by sowing our substance into the Kingdom. Jesus knew that there was a family in that particular village who had a young colt. He also knew that the owners would release it if it was to be used by Him. He knows the men and women who will hold nothing back from Him; He knows those whose hearts (and wallets!) are surrendered to Him.

There are three threads of Truth which we can focus on in this familiar passage of Scripture:

Firstly, Jesus was physically far away, but He knew that the young colt was bound. He sent His disciples with instructions to **untie it. (He came to set the captives free!)**

Secondly, the colt was **freed for a purpose** - the Lord needed it. **He has a plan** for each of us!

Thirdly, freedom leads to fruitfulness when we follow God's plan, and find our own **'Mount of Olives'** where we spend quality time in the presence of our Lord, to rise to higher heights each day!

God desires to minister to you as you read this message today. Like the young colt, there are many precious people who were bound at an early age, and hurt in their minds or bodies. The devil may have had plans to harm and disable us mentally, spiritually or physically, but Jesus came to set the captives free! There may be some colts out there who look perfectly normal, but they are not free. They may even be serving in ministries, but they cannot go further than the length of a rope. The Lord sees and knows your situation. He knows how much you desire to be flying free in the sweetness of His Spirit! From where you are He may seem to be far away, but He is sending help your way. His Word, His servants, His angels have been commissioned to untie those ropes and break the chains. The bad memories, the scars of abuse and sin may have restrained you, but the blood of Jesus speaks on your behalf today! God wants you free; **free to live in the perfect today He has planned for you.** Free to run with open arms into the hope and future which are yours in the Lord. (Jeremiah 29:11).

Jesus said in Matthew 11:28-30 *"Come to me all you who are weary and burdened, and I will give you rest. **Take my yoke upon you and learn from me, for I am gentle and humble in heart, and you will find rest for your souls.** For my yoke is easy and my burden is light."* When the colt was set free, a new life began for him. Jesus took the reigns in His hands, sat upon his back, and guided him in the direction he was to go. That little donkey was not very clever; he was the most humble and insignificant of creatures; but he **submitted to the hand of Jesus** and was used by the King of Kings! He carried Jesus to Jerusalem, and towards the fulfillment of His mission and purpose on the earth - death upon the cross and the salvation of all humanity - that little donkey played a big part in God's plan!

God has higher heights for us all, and a world of blessing that we cannot begin to imagine. However, spiritual victories and new levels of anointing can only come as we tarry in the secret place! The Lord is calling each of us His precious ones into deeper and sweeter communion in His presence. In the same way that Jesus often went away to the Mount of Olives to be alone with God, our Father is calling us to our own Mountain, that secret high place where we will taste of His presence and hear His voice, and know the very beating of His heart! We have been freed for fruitfulness, and this begins to take shape as the healing, cleansing waters of His Word and His Spirit begin to flow into our souls and make us whole. The Lord gives each of us the same invitation He gave to His Apostle John (Revelations 4:1): *"....Come up here...."!* Higher places await us as we begin to climb the mountain.

Finally, we cannot forget the owners of the little colt. They were simple village people, and may not have had great means. A donkey was a valuable asset and the general method of transport in those days. They had not even ridden it, but they had no problem with giving their best and newest to the Lord. It was sufficient for them to know that He needed it! It is significant that in the previous paragraphs, Jesus had been teaching about the ten talents and the importance of making the most of what we have been given. These people knew that the best investment they could make was in the Kingdom. They probably reaped a great harvest!

Let the hand of God come upon you today, as you decide to give your best to Jesus and see His purposes fulfilled. He has set you free and has great plans for you. As you step aside daily into the quiet rest of God's presence and climb up to a higher place, you will begin to see great fruitfulness and anointing flowing through your life! His Word shall come to pass!

May you walk in **Freedom** and in **Fruitfulness,** and **Flow** in the plans and purposes God has for you!

Notes:

Chapter Seven

The Bringer of Peace
(Luke 19:35-44)

"They brought it (the colt) to Jesus, threw their cloaks on the colt and put Jesus on it. As He went along, people spread their cloaks on the road. When He came near the place where the road goes down the Mount of Olives, the whole crowd of disciples began joyfully to praise God in loud voices for all the miracles they had seen. "Blessed is the King who comes in the name of the Lord!" "Peace in Heaven and glory in the highest!"

Some of the Pharisees in the crowd said to Jesus, "Teacher, rebuke your disciples!" "I tell you," He replied, "if they keep quiet, the stones will cry out." As He approached Jerusalem and saw the city, He wept over it and said, "If you, even you, had only known on this day what would bring you peace - but now it is hidden from your eyes. The days will come upon you when your enemies will build an embankment against you and encircle you and hem you in on every side. They will dash you to the ground, you and the children within your walls. They will not leave one stone on another, because you did not recognize the time of God's coming to you."

The last message looked at how Jesus asked His disciples to bring Him a colt to ride on, as He travelled into Jerusalem. This chapter focuses on how the Lord Jesus rode that colt into Jerusalem. It is an evocative description of how people rejoiced in His presence. They praised Him, and acknowledged Him as the 'King', and as the one who came 'in the name of the Lord'!

If we pictured one of the grand and glorious kings of the day, we would see him travel on a strong and mighty horse, decked out in fine purple cloth, bells and shiny amulets. The king himself would have sat regally upon the lofty horse, dressed in satin and velvet, with jewels upon his body and a crown on his head. A red carpet may have been laid before him, for his horse to walk upon, and a herald would run ahead of him, calling out for people to clear the way, bow down on either side of the road, and acknowledge the presence of the king as he came along. This was not so with the Lord Jesus. He was the King of all creation, but He rode a humble little colt. He was the glorious Son of God Almighty and the owner of the universe, but He wore no finery or jewelry. There was no red carpet for Him to ride upon, but the cloaks of those who worshipped Him and acknowledged His Lordship.

The One who walked the streets of gold sat not on fine silk and velvet, but on the garments of His disciples, as He rode into Jerusalem in perfect submission to His father's will. It was all happening as it was meant to be. Over 400 years before the birth of Jesus, the Prophet Zechariah prophesied (Zechariah 9:9-10) *"Rejoice greatly, O Daughter of Zion! Shout, Daughter of Jerusalem! See, your king comes to you, righteous and having salvation, gentle and riding on a donkey, on a colt, the foal of a donkey. I will take away the chariots from Ephraim and the war horses from Jerusalem, and the battle bow will be broken. He will proclaim peace to the nations. His rule will extend from sea to sea and from the River to the ends of the earth."* Jesus comes as the **bringer of peace.** He is the only answer to the problems that nations and people face today! When Jesus rides into a home, a city, a nation, a heart - He brings peace. He is a bringer of salvation and righteousness. When lives are surrendered to Him, He takes away the weapons and vehicles of warfare and destruction. He brings deliverance from every kind of oppression and bondage, and releases His healing and His perfect peace. He came to "proclaim peace to the nations"!

While all this was happening, the Pharisees took exception to the people praising Jesus and calling Him 'King'. Their hearts were so filled with pride that they were jealous of the praise He received! They refused to acknowledge Jesus as the Messiah because they saw Him as the humble son of a carpenter, when their expectation of the Messiah was the proud and regal king we pictured a minute ago - one who would overcome the enemy with the sword! Jesus shook off their protest, saying that if the people were quiet Creation itself would loudly express praise for God!

The Word of God tells us that as Jesus came ***down*** the Mount of Olives, people remembered the miracles they had seen and praised God in loud voices! The more we humble ourselves the more it is possible for people to see God moving in and through our lives, and the more they will praise Him and give Him glory! When we, like Jesus, get off a high horse and walk in humility before God and man, God is truly exalted. As His name is acknowledged and lifted high, His glory comes down and His power flows; His name alone is glorified! The people blessed the Lord that day, and called Jesus their 'King'. They proclaimed 'peace' and 'glory' in heaven.

There was real joy as Jesus rode down the mountain that day. **He is also a bringer of joy!** We cannot help but be joyful and want to praise Him loudly even as the throngs of people did when they remembered the goodness of God in their lives. Many of us may try hard to cultivate an attitude of joy, but it flows naturally when we begin to remember God's loving kindness in our lives, and begin to thank and praise Him loudly; it becomes an effervescent, unstoppable outpouring which breaks depression and heaviness, dispels every negative thought, and stirs up faith!

The Lord Jesus prophesied over the city of Jerusalem. His heart was filled with grief as He rode down the mountain and approached the city of the people of God - the city He loves. He wept as He saw a prophetic vision of what would happen in the days to come. His heart was grieved as He saw the work of the enemy (the Roman Empire) against His people, and the violence and oppression they would have to endure. He saw the city being completely destroyed - with not "one stone left on another", and all because they did not receive the Bringer of peace. All because they did not recognize the time of God's visitation. The lives of the people were steeped in tradition and ritualism. They believed in 'business as usual' and following the 'program' at any cost! Their hearts were so hardened with pride in their own good works that they were unable to recognize Jesus as the Messiah and the Son of God who came to set them free, the One who came from Heaven to earth because of love.

This is a prophecy for churches and ministries at large. It is a prophecy for nations. It is also a Word for those who are experiencing defeat and oppression, and feel they are unable to lift up their heads against the problems coming against them. God is calling us to humble ourselves and heed His voice; to acknowledge His visitation upon our lives and homes, our churches and ministries. He seeks that we recognize His presence and His Lordship, and allow His Spirit the freedom to move in His way. He desires that we stop trying to do things *our* way, and **surrender instead to His Lordship over us**. This is when we begin to see the breakthrough and experience His peace. Let it not be hidden from our eyes dear friend. Jesus said *'If you had only known what* *would bring you peace....'!* We suffer needlessly simply because we have not recognized the opportunities God gave us to know Him better and have His hand upon our lives! We have not recognized the people He sent to us who were anointed to bring us into His blessing and His healing grace, or take us to a higher level in our spiritual walk. We need to welcome His entry into our hearts and homes, into our workplaces and our daily lives; we need to welcome His presence in our churches and ministries, and into our communities and cities. This means welcoming everything that Jesus stands for - not only His love and His mercy, but also His holiness and His chastening; His shaping hand working upon our lives to conform us into the image of the Father. This means abandoning every tradition and ritual and allowing His sweet Spirit to manifest as He wills. We need to surrender everything to Him and allow Him free access to change what He wishes to change, no matter how painful that may be to our flesh! It means truly enthroning Jesus as Lord over every part of our lives, and it can only begin with you and I - those who profess His name and own Him as their Savior. He is the Prince of Peace, He is King and Lord!

It is interesting that the disciples, as well as the people on the streets laid down their cloaks for Jesus to sit on, and ride over. In that day and culture, a person's cloak was considered something of great value. It was often the only means of warmth when it was cold, or protection from the hot desert sun. People even used their cloaks as security for a debt. God calls us to lay down before Him what we con-

sider most precious; the time we spend in some lei-
sure activity, our dependence on family and friends,
our business or career. Are we able to lay aside for
Jesus what is most important to us? It is only when
we let go of any idol we still cling to and humble
ourselves before Him that we can truly surrender to
the Prince of Peace and receive His holy visitation
upon our lives.

May you surrender to the Prince of Peace and
the Bringer of Joy as He rides into your life today.
May you see every enemy vanquished, and the peace
and power of the Lord filling you. He has plans to
prosper you!

Notes:

Chapter Eight

Eye Check (Luke 11:34-36)

"Your eye is the lamp of your body. When your eyes are good, your whole body also is full of light. But when they are bad, your body also is full of darkness. See to it then, that the light within you is not darkness. Therefore, if your whole body is full of light, and no part of it dark, it will be completely lighted, as when the light of a lamp shines on you."

Hidden in this little passage is a secret to spiritual victory, and physical and mental health! May the Holy Spirit minister to you as you read.

We see from the preceding parts of the book of Luke that Jesus taught His disciples about various aspects of Kingdom life; He spoke about love, prayer, spiritual warfare etc. Then He taught them that if their eyes were *'good'* their bodies would be *'full of light'*, but if their eyes were *'bad'*, they would be covered in *'darkness'*!

It is true that life without our physical eyes would be very difficult and painful. For a person with perfect vision, it would be impossible to imagine living a normal life without sight in both eyes. However, there are many people today who live a productive and healthy life, even though their physical eyes may not be functioning according to the Creator's specification. We can therefore see that our Lord is not talking about physical sight in this passage, but about the perceptions of a person, and how these can impact and influence our physical, spiritual and mental state.

As we focus on perceptions, there are three aspects we can look at:

1) Attitudes - Our attitudes affect our perceptions. How we **see** people and circumstances can influence our responses and feelings. The Lord desires that our 'eyes' be 'good', so that our whole body will be full of light. This means that God is calling us to have a **positive attitude** always. If we can be thankful for everything, and look on the **bright** side of any situation, it is not difficult to cultivate an attitude of true joy, which nothing can quell!

The Apostle Paul went through more hardship and persecution than most people we can think of. Still, he wrote in Philippians 4:4 *"Rejoice in the Lord always..."*! It is true that the enemy may prepare snares for us daily, and use people to hurt and discourage us. Circumstances may not always turn out according to our expectations, and we may have to face disappointments and rejection regularly. Quite often our prayers may not be answered the way we desire. But look on the bright side - things could be much worse! And rejoice - we belong to Jesus! The bottom line is that He saved and forgave us, and He is doing a new work in us. What could be better than that! Know that *"in all things God works for the good of those who love Him, who have been called according to His purpose."* (Romans 8:28).

Similar to the way a lamp guides our way in the darkness, our attitudes can actually affect the direction our life takes. (*"As a man thinks in his heart, so will he be"* - Proverbs 23:7 KJV). Let us grow up in our walk with the Lord! Let us learn to receive the enabling of the Holy Spirit to walk in joy and peace, and to keep a positive outlook in every situation. This does not mean that challenging situations cannot ever get us down, but if we look up to the Lord and find something to be **thankful** for even in the most painful of circumstances, He will minister to us and lift us up. He will help us keep a positive attitude! This brings health and wholeness to our bodies and life to our souls (Proverbs 14:30 and Proverbs 17:22), and it frustrates the intentions of the devil, who seeks to drag us down and keep us there, too blinded by negativity to see the light. It can become a habit to grumble, and always look on the darker side of situations. This is the attitude most of the people of Israel had, when they travelled through the desert. They refused to see the goodness and mercy of God, and constantly murmured, and spoke against their circumstances and their leaders. They ended up wandering in the desert for 40 years, because they removed themselves from the grace of God and opened the door to the works of darkness. Joy and thankfulness can be our holy healing balm: *"A cheerful heart is good medicine..."* (Proverbs 17:22).

2) Focus - Food is our body's fuel, and what we regularly eat impacts us positively or negatively. In the same way, the priorities we focus on reflect on our bodies and minds, and affect our life and behavior. I have learnt lately to fill myself with what is most important - the Lord and His Word! When asked what the greatest commandment was, the Lord Jesus said to His disciples *"Love the Lord your God with all your heart, with all your soul, with all your mind and with all your strength, and love your neighbor as yourself"*. James called this the 'Royal Law' (James 2:8). It is a commandment which calls for a commitment to love and please the Lord with every aspect of our being. The Lord desires that we look at our lives and assess what we really focus on. Our focus can be seen through those things which occupy the bulk of our thoughts, our time, and the love of our hearts. Watch out - we become like what we worship and meditate on! For example, people who find themselves repeatedly meditating on offences or past hurts, or the infirmities and problems they see around them may find themselves never able to get away from the issues they coped with in the past. We become what we think about, and bring forth what we expect! It is far better to focus on the glorious and wonderful Lord we serve than on the things of this finite and fallible world! I have seen people who thought they were disciples of the Lord Jesus, but turned away from Him because their leader sinned and fell from grace. This would not happen if our focus was on the Lord instead of a human being. As we fix our eyes on Him and seek Him in worship and in His Word, our hearts and lives are transformed to reflect His image, His holiness and His love. He moves our lives into a different direction and a different dimension. As we seek the Lord and His Kingdom as a priority, there is nothing we will lack. *"But seek first His Kingdom and His righteousness, and all these things will be given to you as well."* (Matthew 6:33).

3) Vision - Proverbs 29:18 tells us that *"without a vision the people perish"*. We need a vision to work and pray towards. We need Godly goals to motivate and inspire us. We need to see with our spiritual eyes what God is planning and preparing for us. If we got a glimpse of what God purposes for us, it would make us jump for joy! He has such beautiful plans for each of His children. (Jeremiah 29:11). Many of us may have heard from the Lord through His Word, or through dreams and visions about what He is preparing us for, or in what direction He is taking our lives. However, for those precious people who have never really seen their purpose on this earth, or God's plan for their lives, now is the time to pray and seek His will and His heart for you. When people decide to serve the Lord, they may hastily commit to serve in some ministry without seeking the will of God. Their motives may be good, but the works of the flesh cannot prosper. It is only when we receive God's vision for us that we are able to step forward in the right direction. When you receive God's vision for you, *"your eyes will be good, and your whole body will be full of light. There will be no darkness, because it will be completely lighted, as when the light of a lamp shines on you"*. This is God's heavenly lamp – spiritual insight and revelation, and the guidance of the blessed Holy Spirit. Not only will your heart and life be full of the glorious light of God, but you will be a light for every one God brings across your path. Hallelujah! Your life will be fruitful and a rich blessing to many. Isaiah 43:18 and 19 says *"Forget the former things; do not dwell on the past. **See** I am doing a new thing. Now it springs up; do you not **perceive** it?"!* Your future is going to be much better than your past!

The Lord Jesus says in this passage of Scripture: *"see to it then, that the light within you is not darkness"*. We are not helpless creatures tossed by the winds of the world - we can **decide** to live in the light and not in the darkness! As you receive this Word, and apply it to all areas of your life, I pray that the Holy Spirit, our Helper and Counselor, will come beside you and empower you. The first step is to ask Him to guide your perceptions and help you fix your attitudes, your focus and your vision towards the Lord Jesus and His Kingdom. As you surrender to the Spirit of God, you will see great restoration, miraculous healing, and powerful growth in every aspect of your life, in Jesus' mighty name. Amen!

Notes:

Chapter Nine

Divine Formula
(Luke 22:39-46)

"Jesus went out as usual to the Mount of Olives, and His disciples followed Him. On reaching the place, He said to them, "Pray that you will not fall into temptation." He withdrew about a stone's throw beyond them, knelt down and prayed, "Father, if you are willing, take this cup from me; yet not my will, but yours be done". An angel from heaven appeared to Him and strengthened Him. And being in anguish, He prayed more earnestly, and His sweat was like drops of blood falling to the ground.

When He rose from prayer and went back to the disciples, He found them asleep, exhausted from sorrow. "Why are you sleeping?" He asked them. "Get up and pray so that you will not fall into temptation."

The most simple principles are sometimes the most powerful! As we focus on these few verses of Scripture, there is so much we can learn, as we press on - in this Kingdom walk the Lord Jesus has called us to. This message is about the 'Jesus' formula!

The Lord Jesus walked in the power and anointing of the Holy Spirit. Wherever He went, people were delivered, saved and healed. He exuded the presence and power of God! Jesus had one formula for everything that happened in His life, including His absolute submission to the Father's Plan: Prayer, prayer and prayer!

1) Prayer was the lifestyle of Jesus. We see from this passage that He went *'as usual'* to the Mount of Olives. It was the special place to which He often went, to pray and fellowship with the Father. This was just prior to His arrest and crucifixion. He experienced so much mental and physical agony that He sweated drops of blood; but this did not hinder Him. Instead, He prayed 'more earnestly'.

Jesus often disappeared before and after times of ministry, to get alone with God. It is not possible to experience spiritual growth, obey God, or impact the world, unless prayer is an integral part of our daily lives.

Jesus also constantly interceded for others. We see in John 17 how He prayed for his disciples, as well as for us who were still to know Him. In Luke chapter 22, verses 31 and 32, Jesus said to Peter *"Satan has asked to sift you as wheat, but I have prayed for you, Simon, that your faith may not fail...."*

2) Prayer provides a shield. Jesus told the disciples to pray, *so that* they would not fall into temptation. The disciples knew their own weaknesses and where they were likely to fall. The Lord Jesus asked them to pray for strength and power to overcome the testing times that would come. Satan normally attacks us in an area of weakness, or one in which we may have fallen in the past. This is not something to fear or feel defeated about because *"when we confess our sins, God is faithful and just and will forgive us our sins and purify us from all unrighteousness"* (1 John 5:9). As we look to Jesus, His Spirit enables us to move on from a place of defeat, to a place of overcoming. As we **stay connected to the Father through prayer**, He keeps us from falling.

When Jesus told His disciples to pray that they would not fall into temptation, I believe He was specifically referring to the temptation to be spiritually inactive. At a time when they should have been praying more than ever before, He came back to find them sleeping, and tired out from their own emotions! He had to alert them again to get up and pray *"so that you will not fall into temptation."* Jesus knew that unless we are actively working against the spiritual forces that seek to derail us, we are likely to come under fire! Spiritual inertia in a battle zone is dangerous, and is in itself a trick of the evil one, who uses any tactics to stop intercessors praying! Jesus was talking about the fact that sometimes there seems to be no desire for prayer when the need is greatest.

He is the eternal Intercessor, interceding for us at the right hand of the Father (Romans 8:34, Hebrews 7:25). He is calling His Bride to take her spiritual stand in spiritual authority, and pray. The need is greater now, in these dark days, than ever before. One of us can put a thousand to flight, and two of us ten thousand! We have been given the power to decree and declare God's Kingdom on earth.

3) Jesus got alone with God. Group prayer meetings are wonderful, and very motivating and powerful, but they should never replace time alone with the Father, fellowshipping with Him like Jesus did. As we spend heart to heart time with God, we hear His voice and are refreshed and renewed by His Spirit. We are molded into the image of Jesus, and our hearts become submitted to His will – we receive the mind of Christ! This is how Jesus was able to say "This cup of suffering is going to be bitter and painful, but I want to do what you want; I want to obey you, whatever the cost..."

4) God sent an angel to strengthen Jesus. Jesus knew the purpose for which He had been born upon the earth, and that He was God's plan for the redemption of mankind; but He had to receive prayer power as He battled with His flesh, and asked for strength to stay in the Father's will and go willingly to the cross which was before Him. As He cried out to the Father, God sent an angel to minister to Him and give Him strength to stay with the plan, however hard and painful it was to His humanity. He was strengthened enough to pray with renewed power *("more earnestly")*, sweating blood as spirit battled flesh. If you set your heart to do God's will and walk in His purposes in the face of all the challenges and obstacles that come against you, God will send angels (divine and human!) to help and encourage you on your journey of prayer and obedience. You will never have to walk alone! He will strengthen you physically and spiritually.

Through this passage of Scripture the Lord Jesus shows us that there is no way we can overcome the wiles and weapons of the enemy unless we are **people of purposeful prayer.** Kingdom people have lost so much territory (spiritual and physical) to the powers of darkness because the fire of prayer has not been burning fiercely in our fellowships, our homes, and in our personal walk with God.

In Old Testament times, God decreed that the lamp in the temple was never to go out. It had to be fuelled night and day with fresh oil so that the flame would keep burning brightly always. This is symbolic of prayer and its power. **The oil of the blessed Holy Spirit keeps prayer flowing** with freshness and a divine impact in the spiritual realm. As the presence of the Holy Spirit diminishes in a person or a group, the spirit of prayer begins to dry up too. The lamp eventually goes out unless we open ourselves afresh to the Holy Spirit and stir up the spirit of prayer once more. **There is nothing we can build in the Kingdom without a foundation of prayer.** This is true for us as individuals, as well as for churches and groups. Nations that have come to God and begun to pray in one accord have seen powerful transformation in every aspect of their economies and societies.

Friend, I challenge you to commit to pray for your city and neighborhood, for your church, and the nation in which you live, not just for a day or a week, but as a part of your daily walk with God. God is calling believers everywhere to take their places as watchmen on the walls and pray back the Kingdom into their cities, schools, homes, and places of work. There is a powerful end-time anointing to be released upon the Bride, but she has to make herself ready! Things have to be settled in the spiritual realm before they are ever seen in the physical.

It is only natural that there will be spiritual opposition as we begin to take up the powerful weapon of prayer. But remember as you lift up holy hands and pick up spiritual weapons to pray that Jesus Himself is praying for you! He is seated at the right hand of the Father, interceding on your behalf. He is covering you, and praying that you will stand strong in the power of His Spirit, and stay in the battle. He is praying that you will keep your eyes on Him and not fall into the temptation of complacency, inertia or sin. He is praying that you will pray, and that you will walk the narrow road, finish the race, and hear the Father say "Well done"!

Rise up to receive the commission God has for you. Rise up to take your stand in God's army. You are a person of power and prayer!

Notes:

Chapter Ten

A Miraculous Meal
(John 6:1-13)

"Some time after this, Jesus crossed to the far shore of the Sea of Galilee (that is, the Sea of Tiberias), and a great crowd of people followed Him because they saw the miraculous signs He had performed on the sick. Then Jesus went up on a mountainside and sat down with His disciples. The Jewish Passover Feast was near. When Jesus looked up and saw a great crowd coming towards Him, He said to Philip, "Where shall we buy bread for these people to eat?" He asked this only to test him, for He already had in mind what He was going to do. Philip answered Him, "Eight months' wages would not buy enough bread for each one to have a bite!"

Another of His disciples, Andrew, Simon Peter's brother, spoke up, "Here is a boy with five small barley loaves and two small fish, but how far will they go among so many?"

Jesus said, "Make the people sit down." There was plenty of grass in that place, and the men sat down, about five thousand of them. Jesus then took the loaves, gave thanks, and distributed to those who were seated as much as they wanted. He did the same with the fish.

When they had all had enough to eat, He said to His disciples, "Gather the pieces that are left over. Let nothing be wasted." So they gathered them and filled twelve baskets with the pieces of the five barley loaves left over by those who had eaten."

This passage of Scripture may be a familiar one to many. Most children learn about the 'feeding of the five thousand' in Sunday school. It is a beautiful account of the miraculous provision of God in the lives of His children. There are many powerful truths we can draw from it, to see the same miracle operating in our own lives today!

Thousands of people had witnessed the many miracles that were flowing through the ministry of the Lord Jesus, and crowds followed Him everywhere. Just when Jesus and His disciples thought they had got away to a quiet place to spend some time in fellowship, they saw that they had been followed once more, and it was a large crowd! They were miles from anywhere and Jesus wanted to feed the hungry horde that had sought Him out. We are told that Jesus already knew how He would provide refreshment for this huge crowd, but He tested Philip, saying *"Where shall we buy bread for these people to eat?"*

Friend, believe that however great the need in your life today, the Lord Jesus knows how it will be met. He is able! He may permit us to come to a place where we see no physical means of meeting a payment or seeing a healing we desperately need, and this may cause us to question God and wonder how the problem might be resolved. It may seem like a completely hopeless situation, but remember that every challenge is like a divine test; we can choose to trust God and believe His Word, or believe the report of the world; the fleshly solutions that people offer usually come to naught. Philip had seen the mighty miracle-working power of God flowing through the life and ministry of Jesus; he had seen the exciting and innovative way Jesus worked and lived. He should have expected the impossible and unusual, and believed for it; but he did not pass the test, as was the case with Andrew! Andrew presented the boy with the bread and fish to Jesus, while saying, *"but how far will they go among so many?"* With our minds we may all know that Jesus is able to do the impossible, but when it comes to trusting Him from the heart, we hear ourselves saying *"but how far will it go..."* as human reasoning somehow quells faith, which has to believe before it sees.

We place boundaries on the limitless power of God when we doubt His omnipotence, and perceive Him with the eyes of the flesh, and through its limitations. We need to remember that we serve a mighty

God who is infinite in His power and ability - there is nothing too hard for Him! If we made it our lifestyle to see God in this way, instead of through the spectacle frames of institutionalized religion many of us have grown with, we would understand that nothing is too hard for us. No barrier can stand against us, because He - the Almighty - lives in us, and greater is He who is in us than he that is in the world!

There are four things Jesus did here, which really brought the blessing to pass:

Firstly, He said *"Make the people sit down."* The food was still only five small barley loaves and two small fish, but He **believed** that when He asked His Father, this miniscule quantity of food would be sufficiently multiplied to feed that multitude. It all boils down to **faith**. In the world we see to believe, but in the Kingdom, we **believe to see!** May I challenge you, precious child of God, to take the biggest need in your life and bring it to God, and then begin to live your life as though it was already coming to pass. The people were asked to sit down on the grass in anticipation of the meal which was to come!

Secondly, Jesus gave thanks for what He had in His hands! We are often so busy grumbling about what we do not have that we fail to see the awesome blessing we already have in our hands! To see favor and increase in our lives, our substance, our ministries, our careers, relationships etc, let us begin to be thankful to God for what we already have! How many of us would want to do more for someone who never appreciated what we had already done for them? Jesus lifted up those five small loaves and the two small fish and gave thanks to God. He had these in His hands because a young boy obeyed the tug of the Holy Spirit upon His heart. The Lord Jesus gave thanks not only for what He already had in His hands, but He thanked God in faith for the increase that was to come. The boy offered it to Jesus, and Jesus offered it all to the Father in faith. Hebrews 11:1 says that *"Faith is being sure of what we hope for and certain of what we do not see"*. Faith enables us to see in the spirit what has not yet manifested in the flesh. Faith believes the Word of God is true, and that it is fulfilled, regardless of the physical signs to the contrary. It is as we believe for it and take it that we begin to see with our physical eyes what God has blessed us with.

Thirdly, Jesus began to break that small quantity of fish and bread and distribute it. Friend, whatever you believe you lack in your life, that is the very thing God is asking you to share and pass on to bless another life. It may be time, money, love, ministry or friendships. Whatever it may be, the principle of sowing and reaping operates. It is what you give that you will receive back in blessed abundance! I believe that the food was multiplied to such an extent because the pieces were passed on, broken, and passed on. The Lord passed pieces on to His disciples, who broke them and passed them on, and each person broke and passed on, until every person in that colorful multitude was amply fed. They even gathered twelve basketfuls of pieces after all had eaten, because the Master hates waste. What a powerful picture!

Fourthly, Jesus kept the right focus. Philip and Andrew focused on the wrong thing - they were looking at the enormity of the need, rather than at the greatness of God. This is what the devil would have us do. He desires that we focus on the size of the problem against the smallness of our means. He wants us to think that a disease is incurable, or that debts can never be repaid; but for us, the chosen of the Lord, the story does not end here! We are more than conquerors through Him who loves us. Jesus has made it possible for us to overcome! When Jesus lifted up those loaves and looked up to Heaven, He focused on the source of the blessing. If we keep our eyes on the problem or the things of the world, we may never see the miracle we are seeking. But as we look upwards and beyond, and focus on Heaven, where there is no sickness, lack or oppression, our faith is strengthened to see Heaven move and bring to earth the very thing we are longing for.

It is worth noting that the people had *"as much as they wanted".* God never rations the blessings He pours out on His children. In many places in the Word of God, we see that the blessing continued to flow for as long as people continued to draw upon it and receive. There is no limit to what God can do – only the limitations in our own faith to believe for something big! Too often we approach God with the same attitude we may have when we seek the help of a human friend – hesitantly, and trying to ensure that we do not make too big a demand or impose too much on their time and resources. We also would never want a friend to think we took advantage of their kindness or took them for granted. However, the opposite is true when it comes to seeking God's help. The reality is that our indulgent Father God, our El Shaddai, really does want us to take advantage of His kindness and love; He wants us to believe in His goodness and mercy, and trust in the richness of His omnipotent power. He can; He will; He is Infinite God!

Dear Friend, this same miracle is available to each of us. If we cultivate a **lifestyle of faith, thankfulness, and giving,** and if we **focus on the things of God,** we can see God do mighty things in our lives. The passage talks about the fact that the *'Jewish Passover Feast was near.* It is significant that the Gospel writer mentions this.

The Feast of Passover was first celebrated in Egypt, when the angel of God **passed over** the sons of Israel and smote the first born of the Egyptians. **Three days later** at the Red Sea, the Jews **passed through** the waters parted by God and arrived safely on the other side, no longer slaves to Pharaoh. On Passover, about 32 AD, judgment **passed over** us, the chosen, and smote instead the only begotten Son of God. **Three days later,** Jesus rose from the dead and the chosen **passed through** from the penalty of death into eternal life.

Jesus is the Passover *"Lamb who takes away the sin of the world* (John 1:29). He is *"Christ, our Passover lamb who has been sacrificed"* (1 Corinthians 5:7). Jesus is the perfect lamb without blemish, *"but was in all points tempted as we are, yet without sin"* (Heb 4:15). He is our substitutionary atonement: *"For God made Him who had no sin to be sin for us, so that in Him we might become the righteousness of God"* (2 Corinthians 5:21).

It is only through the sweet Passover Lamb that we can enter into the fullness of Blessing that God has in store for those who become His. Are you washed in the blood of the Lamb? Have you passed over from death to life? Are you a joint heir with Jesus Christ, of all the abundance and goodness that has already been released in the Heavens for you and me? If you have partaken of the Passover Lamb, you are a child of the King; you belong to God, and through the Power of the Holy Spirit, you will see all the fullness of His glory manifested in your life!

May every situation of lack be broken from your life, and may God **gloriously** and **abundantly** supply every need, as you believe in **His mighty power** and **His amazing love. Remember – as you believe, you will receive!**

Notes:

Chapter Eleven

Over The Storms
(Luke 8:22-25)

"One day Jesus said to His disciples, "Let's go over to the other side of the lake." So they got into a boat and set out. As they sailed, He fell asleep. A squall came down on the lake, so that the boat was being swamped, and they were in great danger. The disciples went and woke Him, saying, "Master, Master, we're going to drown!"

He got up and rebuked the wind and the raging waters; the storm subsided, and all was calm. "Where is your faith?" He asked His disciples. In fear and amazement they asked one another, "Who is this? He commands even the winds and the water, and they obey Him."

The Lord Jesus and His disciples were rowing across the Sea of Galilee. This is actually a large freshwater lake through which the Jordan River flows. (The Jordan enters at the north end of the Sea of Galilee, near where Jesus lived, at Capernaum, and flows out southward through the Jordan Valley to the Salt Sea). The lake is 13 miles long and 8 miles wide. It can be the scene of powerful storms that happen suddenly when dry, cold air from the surrounding heights flows down to collide with the moist, warmer air over the lake.

We are told that Jesus fell asleep in the boat. He was probably very weary, after a heavy day of teaching His disciples and ministering the power of God. While the Lord was asleep, a violent storm began to rage, and the boat was shaken and knocked about. It felt to the disciples as though the situation was out of control; they feared for their lives!

It is interesting to note from the next account in this same chapter of the book of Luke that when the group reached the opposite shore of the lake, the Lord Jesus ministered to (and set free) a man who had been bound by many demons! The man who had been seen to manifest self destructive, suicidal behavior for many years suddenly came into posses-sion of his mind and became a new person! It was a miracle of deliverance by the power of God. This man had been bound for many years and had lived in uncleanness and darkness. He had lived under a spirit of death and decay - in the tombs, but when the Lord Jesus reached out and ministered life to him, he was set free!

Friend, there was a reason for this storm. When you decide to 'cross the lake' and go over to the 'other side', there is usually a level of opposition. When you desire to obey the calling of God, and decide to step into ministry, it is likely that unexpected storms will suddenly break out. It is the same when you get tired of where you are in your walk with the Lord and you hunger for more. When you begin to seek more of God and His Spirit, storms may break out to discourage you and stop you in your tracks. Whenever the Lord is moving you from where you are and taking you to a different level, you can be sure that there will be 'storms' to overcome. But rejoice! When the Lord Jesus tells us to go somewhere, He is always with us in the boat. He is the name above every name. He is over the storms that come against us. No weapon formed against us shall prosper!

Luke tells us that the disciples panicked when the storm was swirling around them! They anticipated and believed the worst possible scenario. They woke Jesus saying *"we are going to drown"!* When you feel like all hell is breaking lose against you, you can choose to do one of the following:

1) Remember that Jesus is in the boat, and trust Him to take you through the storm. He has promised that He will never leave us *("Never will I leave you; never will I forsake you."* Hebrews 13:5). God said to His people (Isaiah 43:2 & 4) *"When you pass through the waters I will be with you; and when you pass through the rivers, they will not sweep over you. When you walk through the fire you will not be burned; the flames will not set you ablaze."* When the enemy comes against us like an overwhelming flood, the blessed Holy Spirit will rise up on our behalf (Isaiah 59:19) and contend with our attackers (Isaiah 50:8).

Or :

2) Give in to fear and anticipate the worst. Very often, this unhappy scenario could possibly be what happens, because it is what we have been believing for! Just as the wonderful blessings and miracles of God can come to pass in our lives because they are what we have faith for, the same is true of the unpleasant and painful things the devil plans for the children of God when we believe for them! We may sometimes even speak our fears aloud, not paying attention to the fact that words are potent and impacting. (Proverbs 18:21 - *"The tongue has the power of life and death, and those who love it will eat its fruit."*) The evil one and his angels are quick to take our words and bring them to fulfillment.

On the other hand, when we choose to believe and proclaim God's Word, and stand on it even in the face of adverse evidence, the angels of God bring His Word to powerful and miraculous fulfillment. This has been my experience time and again.

Although the disciples panicked and gave in to fear, **they did something right; they cried out to the Master.** They woke Him up and called Him to action. And what action they saw! The Lord Jesus showed them His mastery - even over the wind and the foaming waves and all the powers of the enemy.

He commanded the spirits manipulating the elements to be still, and they bowed down to the voice of Jesus, because every knee must bow, and every tongue confess His Lordship. The waters became calm, and the winds died down because Jesus is the mighty ruler of the universe! You may be facing a difficult situation and feeling as though Jesus is 'asleep' in the boat. The storm may be raging around you, with a battle front in more than one aspect of your life. It is time to cry out, and call on the name of Jesus. God has promised that even when we pass through the darkest valley, He will be with us (Psalm 23:4: *"Even though I walk through the valley of the shadow of death, I will fear no evil, for You are with me; Your rod and Your staff they comfort me."*) He is with us and He hears us when we call. He is Almighty God – there is nothing too hard for Him!

Jesus said to His disciples *'where is your faith?'* They had walked closely with the Lord for many months now. They had seen His power and authority over sickness, death and demons, and still, when faced with this unexpected situation, they fell apart! Christians often believe that all their troubles will go away when they become disciples of the Lord Jesus. In fact, our challenges usually increase soon after we become a part of the Kingdom, because we become the enemy of the powers we used to be subject to. People are frequently discouraged and disappointed when their lives are hit by unexpected storms, and they may even step out of the boat and walk away from a life with Jesus. The Lord Jesus never promised us a bed of roses! He said to His disciples (in John 16:33) *"In this world you will have trouble. But take heart! I have overcome the world."* Instead of focusing on the fact that we will (and do) face trials in our life on this troubled earth, we can remember that **our Master has already overcome whatever storms the devil could ever raise up against us**. Storms may come our way or rage within our hearts, but He is able to turn them all around. **Jesus can transform the worst situation to peace.** Hallelujah!

Friend, God has good plans for His children, and we should live in the positive expectation of His goodness and favor upon our lives. However, if circumstances turn out contrary to our expectations, we cannot panic and bow down to fear. The One who commands even the winds and the waters is within us. He is with us in the boat! We could allow the battles of life to weaken us and fill us with fear and negative anticipation; or we can see these as occasions to strengthen our faith muscles and grow in our relationship with God. He is faithful and trustworthy. He will always cause us to triumph.

I pray that you will **choose to take the way of faith and not the way of fear.** The disciples saw Jesus conquer the storm before they said in amazement and awe *"He commands even the wind and the water and they obey Him...!"* The next time you are faced with an unexpected storm, remember that the Lord is really with you. Call on the name of Jesus in the assurance of faith and in the understanding that in Him, you **will** always be victorious! Remember that the devil will do everything to stop you getting to the other side of the lake, but if you look to God and persist, there is a greater anointing, greater authority, and victory over every dark power that comes against you. The enemy will begin to step back as you approach! You and the Lord Jesus are a majority, and He is with you in your boat!

Notes:

Chapter Twelve

Loving The "Jesus" Way (Matthew 5:43-48)

"You have heard that it was said, 'Love your neighbor and hate your enemy.' But I tell you: Love your enemies and pray for those who persecute you, that you may be sons of your Father in heaven. He causes His sun to rise on the evil and the good, and sends rain on the righteous and the unrighteous. If you love those who love you, what reward will you get? Are not even the tax collectors doing that? And if you greet only your brothers, what are you doing more than others? Do not even pagans do that? Be perfect therefore, as your heavenly Father is perfect."

None of the instructions the Lord Jesus gave us, His disciples, are easy! The very nature of what He has commanded us to do makes it impossible for us to obey unless we remember that we 'can do all things through Christ who strengthens us'! (Philippians 4:13).

In Old Testament times, the law prescribed 'an eye for an eye and a tooth for a tooth'. Revenge was quite acceptable so long as people paid in 'kind' for what they did to someone else, and both parties were 'quits' at the end of the day! However, the Lord Jesus is calling us to go against the grain. This passage of Scripture tells us to do the opposite of what comes naturally to the human frame. We instinctively tend to return negative for negative, and positive for positive. It would seem natural to be kind to those who have been pleasant and nice to us, whereas we may keep away from, or think badly of those who have left us with a bitter memory! In our hearts, we may even vaguely wish 'someone' would 'teach them a lesson', and bring them to repentance and remorse for what they did to us! This sounds very childish but it is often true.

The Lord Jesus Christ is asking us to do in His strength what we cannot possibly do in ours:

1) To stop feeling sorry for ourselves because of wrongs done to us.
2) To stop dwelling on the bad or unpleasant experience we have had.
3) To stop considering how we can get 'even' with the person who hurt us.
4) To go a further mile and begin to sow an investment of prayer and blessing upon the lives of those who caused us pain.
5) To stay in relationship with them.

Almost impossible!

Jesus said here that it is not a great achievement if we love only those who love us, or if we maintain relationships only with those who are 'nice' to us. This is something anyone is capable of doing in their own strength. In the days of Jesus, the tax collectors were perceived as dishonest, sinners, and traitors to the nation. They were seen as spiritually far away from the requirements of God, and not the most socially acceptable people at the time. Jesus said that even they knew to relate positively to those who related well to them. But Jesus set us a higher standard. He asked us to be different. He said that if we claim to be His followers, we need to be like Him. If we claim to be the children of God, we need to be like our Heavenly Father, who universally pours out many blessings on many people, even those who reject Him and revile His name. This is the love of God! Paul wrote in 1 Corinthians 13:1 *'If I speak in the tongues of men and of angels, but have not love, I am only a resounding gong or a clanging cymbal. If I have the gift of prophecy and can fathom all mysteries and all knowledge, and if I have a faith that can move mountains, but have not love, I am nothing. If I give all I possess to the poor and surrender my body to the flames, but have not love, I gain nothing.'* And in 1 Corinthians 13:5 *'love keeps no record of wrongs....'* True Love is not easy!

We can see that our walk of love is more important to the Father, than any service we could give Him or any ministries or gifts we operate in. It is true that

God's name is glorified when we operate in the gifts of the Spirit, but there is no greater glory given to our Lord than when His children walk in His love! God's love takes humility; God's love takes surrender to the Spirit; God's love is tough - it takes an overcomer to love as Jesus asks us to!

One night, my family was travelling back from a Christian conference we attended in Texas, where we were all renewed and refreshed in the Holy Spirit, and experienced a powerful anointing. Our flight back to Washington DC was a late night one - and we were all very tired. The Lord warned us before we left our hotel for a few strenuous hours of hot and sticky sightseeing that the enemy would attempt to disturb and spoil the beautiful joy of the fresh anointing we had received. This came to pass! We had a bad experience on the flight back, with a very rude flight attendant, who did not seem to understand that we live in a customer driven market! As I sat back and shut my eyes, I called on the Lord and asked Him for grace to be silent in the face of unexpected provocation. My mind went to an account in 2 Kings 2:23-24 where Elisha called down a curse on some people who were cruel to him, and how bears came out of the woods and mauled the people! I then thought with some relish that I could write a strong letter to the airline, telling them about the conduct of their employee. However, suddenly these words flashed into my heart, *'love your enemies and pray for those who persecute you'* (Matthew 5:44). And also *'your battle is not with flesh and blood'* (Ephesians 6:12). After all, the Lord had already warned us to be on the alert! I was reminded afresh that in this awe-some walk we enjoy with our Savior, we are called to face the persecutions He faced and still walk like He did; to love like He loves, and to respond as He responded when He hung upon the cross and said *"Father forgive them, for they know not what they do"*. I was also reminded that love is really a form of spiritual warfare. The enemy has no response to love - his language is bitterness, anger, and unforgiveness, which ultimately poisons the victim more than the trespasser, if they allow themselves to be consumed by it.

This was not some trivial experience, but one of deep correction for me from the hand of our Father who is committed to molding us into His image. We all face many challenging experiences from day to day, when we can choose to fall into the trap of the evil one, and react in anger and revenge, or at the very least, to continue to simmer in a state of low grade resentment, which allows the bitterness to slowly gather substance and burst out later. Or we can choose to switch our thoughts away from self pity and wallowing in the issue, and begin to invest blessing and prayer upon the life of the very person who caused us pain!

Children are normally expected to reflect the nature of their parents, and we may often know the kind of family in which a person grew up, or what their parents are like from the way they relate to people and situations. God says *"Love your enemies and pray for those who persecute you, that you may be **sons** of your Father in heaven."* He wants people to see Him in us! He wants the world to want to know Him because they see His love in us. When we walk in His love, we are reflecting the image of Jesus – the one who said *"Greater love has no one than this, that He lay down His life for His friends."* (John 15:13). God is calling us to break out of the norms of the world and walk in the radical love that He did.

Jesus said *'be perfect as your Heavenly Father is perfect!'* He was talking about spiritual maturity – the revelation of the impossible becoming possible because the friend of God has learnt how to rest in Him! And remember that *"in this world you will have trouble, but do not fear for He has overcome the world"* (John 16:33). May the Almighty give you grace and strength in your time of need - to follow the Spirit and not the flesh, and to show this world that God is real and His love is great. Be filled with the power of God's love and remember that you can walk as Jesus did – He enables you!

Notes:

Chapter Thirteen

A Mustard Seed
(Luke 17:5-6)

"The apostles said to the Lord, "Increase our faith!" He replied, "If you have faith as small as a mustard seed, you can say to this mulberry tree, "Be uprooted and planted in the sea," and it will obey you".

Also Matthew 17:20: *"I tell you the truth, if you have faith as small as a mustard seed, you can say to this mountain, "Move from here to there" and it will move. Nothing will be impossible to you."*

This chapter is about something we would all like more of - **faith!** Hebrews 11:1 describes faith as *'being sure of what we hope for and certain of what we do not see'*. Faith is all about a choice we make, either to believe the Word of God, or to believe and act upon the signs that are before our eyes; to stand on what cannot yet be physically seen, and not be flattened by the mountain that we can see! It is a tough choice but one we make, consciously or unconsciously, in every situation in life. As we look at the giants of faith in God's Word and in the Kingdom today, the kind of faith we see in their lives may be what we all desire. As the disciples did, I too asked God many times to increase my faith, until He gave me the revelation I needed to see it happen!

The disciples of the Lord asked Him to increase their faith, and their desire sounds very good and spiritual. They probably thought Jesus would lay His hand upon their heads and impart more faith into them. The Lord Jesus' reply was not what they expected; He said that they could begin to do mighty miracles **if** they had the smallest amount of faith. It is clear that the level of our faith is our responsibility and our choice. But how do we begin? With a mustard seed! Jesus gave us the key:

Jesus said in Luke 13:18 to 20 *"What is the Kingdom of God like? What shall I compare it to? It is like a mustard seed, which a man took and planted in his garden. It grew and became a tree, and the birds of the air perched in its branches. Again He asked, 'What shall I compare the Kingdom of God to? It is like yeast that a woman took and mixed into a large amount of flour until it worked all through the dough."* Here's the mustard seed again! The Kingdom is all about faith. We access it only by faith and nothing happens in the Kingdom apart from faith. In fact, the Word of God tells us that everything that does not come from faith is sin (Romans 14:23).

"And without faith it is impossible to please God..." (Hebrews 11:6).

We started with the little seed of faith we experienced when God the Holy Spirit moved upon us and enabled us to believe for salvation in Jesus. God gave to each one of us a measure of faith (Romans 12:3). We had faith for the forgiveness of sins. That was the first little mustard seed, but the open door to all the riches of Heaven! In Luke 13, Jesus also compared the Kingdom to a little bit of yeast which was mixed into flour to become a large amount of dough. **He is talking about increase**. Just as our physical bodies become stronger and grow when we eat the right food and exercise regularly, so also our faith increases when we feed our spirits the Word of God, and when we exercise our faith, believing God for progressively greater things. **Faith grows progressively.** As God began to show me this, I began to take Him seriously; I began to feed myself the Word of God like never before. I began to exercise my faith - choosing to trust His Word in unexpected situations instead of giving in to fear, or looking for human solutions. My faith is certainly growing, and I believe the same can happen for you!

Remember, however, that your faith will not normally expand overnight! Another relevant Kingdom principle here is that of seed time and harvest. The mustard seed does not become a tree overnight. (There is a time for sown seeds to grow, and a time to harvest them). In Genesis 8:22, God made a promise to Noah and He said *"As long as the earth endures, seed **time** and harvest....."* As you sow the Word of

God into your life, and give it **time** to grow, you will eventually reap a harvest of great faith which will enable you to believe for the impossible! And all along the way, you will see yourself being able to believe for progressively greater things as your faith grows.

Start with what you have. It may be difficult to trust God for the resurrection of a dead relative if we have not exercised faith for the healing of a cold. However, just as Jesus taught His disciples, He is telling us today that it is up to us - we can make it or break it! We can choose to believe God's Word today and have faith for our faith to grow. The mustard seed is said to be the smallest seed we could find, but it grows into a great tree. Faith is the same. Feed the mustard seed of faith, water it with the Word, exercise it, and see awesome Kingdom miracles flowing in and through your life. Your life will become a place of healing and rest for others, just as Jesus told His disciples in Luke 13 – *"It grew and became a tree and the birds of the air perched in its branches"*. You will also be a source of life, strength, and spiritual food, as was the small quantity of yeast which brought forth much dough and then bread.

Many precious people of God struggle with long term problems like addictions, compulsions, uncontrollable thoughts, or oppressive dreams. These may exist because of generational issues which are deeply rooted like the mulberry tree the Lord Jesus refers to in Luke 17:6. However, even these deep roots have to come out when we approach them with **faith.** They will be removed and cast into the sea, because **all**

things are possible to those who **believe.** If we chose to focus on the size of the tree and how long it has lived in the ground and borne bitter fruit, then we may never see it rooted out; but if we stand on God's Word, and receive the words which Jesus said in Matthew 15:13 (*"Every plant that my heavenly Father has not planted will be pulled up by the roots"*), and attack the roots with faith-filled fasting and prayer, that evil plant is coming right out! Hallelujah!

Friend, if you begin to work at increasing your faith, you will see that Jesus was right when He said in Matthew 17:21 that *"Nothing will be impossible for you"* or in Luke 9:23 *"All things are possible for him who believes"!* You will see growth and overcoming in every aspect of your life and ministry, your health and finances, your relationships, and your impact on the lives of others. All things will be possible as you pray in faith! Faith will be the foundation and practice of your whole life.

May the blessed Holy Spirit enable you to grow stronger in your faith each day. Be consistent, and keep doing what you have to do, and you will see the power of God exploding around you like never before. The mountains that stood impassable before you **will** move, and it all starts with a mustard seed! This is what God wants for you!

Notes:

Chapter Fourteen

Resurrection Power
(Luke 7:11-17)

"Soon afterwards, Jesus went to a town called Nain, and His disciples and a large crowd went along with Him. As He approached the town gate, a dead person was being carried out - the only son of his mother, and she was a widow. And a large crowd from the town was with her. When the Lord saw her, His heart went out to her and He said, "Don't Cry." Then He went up and touched the coffin, and those carrying it stood still. He said, "Young man, I say to you, get up!" The dead man sat up and began to talk, and Jesus gave him back to his mother. They were all filled with awe and praised God. "A great prophet has appeared among us," they said. "God has come to help His people." This news about Jesus spread throughout Judea and the surrounding country."

Why did Jesus go to this little town called Nain? Only because there was a divine appointment! It is possible to picture the funeral procession Jesus and His companions met, as they approached the town. Eastern people are very expressive in their mourning of the dead. The procession probably included a flute player and a drummer, while the people cried aloud, beating their chests and hitting their heads as they went along. The whole town (it was 'a large crowd') was probably walking alongside the coffin. The people all mourned the tragedy of a young man cut off in his prime, doubly sad because he was the only child of a widow. She was a grief-stricken mother! How she must have wept and cried aloud when she saw that he was dead, and there was no more hope.... or that is what she thought. She was alone in the world, and in a patriarchal culture and time where women had little education or skills, she had few choices for her survival.

However, God had a different plan! When Jesus saw the grief of the weeping mother, and the other mourners, He felt her pain. He was filled with divine compassion. In the power and unstoppable conviction of the Holy Spirit He approached the group. Such glory must have been upon His face - such fiery, Heavenly purpose - that the procession stopped; this was a 'God' moment! We are told that the Lord's heart went out to the mother of the boy, as He comforted her, saying 'don't cry'! Jesus knew what was to come. He wanted that lady to stop weeping and wailing over a death which was soon to be annulled! Death could not continue to have a hold when the

Master came on the scene! Jesus walked to the coffin and touched it. This probably shocked the people; according to Old Testament Law, anyone who touched a dead body immediately became 'unclean' (Numbers 19:1-22 and Leviticus 21:1). This was not a matter of concern to Jesus, because in His sight, the boy was not dead but alive. He is Lord over everything. Jesus spoke to the corpse. He addressed the boy and commanded him to get up! And because Jesus - **the Word** - speaks louder than the voice of death, disease, and destruction, the boy's spirit returned; he sat up and spoke. He had a lot to talk about – of all the inexpressible things in the other dimension he had visited. He had experienced his spirit leaving his body; he had stepped outside of time and space into eternity. But at the command of the King of kings and Lord of lords, his spirit returned and he was reunited with his mother. This lady, who had been grieving and sick to the heart a moment before, was suddenly celebrating – her son was alive, awake, and back in her arms! Glory came down!

Luke reports that the people were filled with awe. They knew this was an act of God, for who else has power over life and death but Almighty God. They believed that God had worked through the life of a great prophet to bring life back to this boy. They said 'God has come to help His people'.

From this passage we can see two reasons why God raises the dead: **Firstly, that His name may be glorified,** and that people will see Him for who He is. **Secondly,** because His heart is filled with **compassion** when He sees the grief and pain of His people.

When a person dies prematurely, we can believe for a supernatural intervention of God - that the same Spirit who raised Jesus from the dead, can in power bring life back to the person who died! If only we could all begin to **believe** for such acts of power as a regular part of our lives, we would see God do the same thing through our lives as we speak life into dead bones and cause them to live as the Prophet Ezekiel did!

Death came to destroy and devour from this family in Nain, but Jesus is triumphant over death and the devourer! He said *"The thief comes only to steal, kill and destroy; but I have come that they may have life and have it to the full."* Fullness of life is what we can expect as the children of God (John 10:10). Jesus said to the grieving sister of Lazarus before He raised him from the dead (John 11:25) *"I am the resurrection and the life..."*. Neither Death nor the grave could hold the Lord Jesus down. He defeated Death! He rose from the grave on the third day, and because of His victory over death, He speaks to Death even today, and brings it under His Holy feet. Every knee must bow, and every tongue confess that Jesus Christ is Lord. Death has to bow its knee in the presence and at the command of the Lord of all, who threw off the shackles of the grave.

Friend, it does not matter how 'dead' your situation may seem to be – God can reverse it, and turn it around, in the same way He resurrected the young man from Nain. We serve a God of power and might, for whom **nothing** is impossible! I pray that you will seek the face of God and believe for a miracle. He sees your pain and His heart overflows with compassion for you. Today He looks into your heart and says (as He said to the mother from Nain) *"my precious child, trust me - don't cry"*. There is resurrection power in His presence and that power is available to you today!

Notes:

Chapter Fifteen

Walking On Water
(Matthew 14:22-27)

"Immediately Jesus made the disciples get into the boat and go on ahead of Him to the other side, while He dismissed the crowd. After He had dismissed them, He went up on a mountainside by Himself to pray. When evening came, He was there alone, but the boat was already a considerable distance from land, buffeted by the waves because the wind was against it.

During the fourth watch of the night, Jesus went out to them, walking on the lake. When the disciples saw Him walking on the lake, they were terrified. "It's a ghost," they said, and cried out in fear. But Jesus immediately said to them: "Take courage! It is I. Don't be afraid."

The Lord Jesus had just spent most of the night in prayer, and it was the fourth (and last) watch of the night. The four Jewish watches of the night were three hourly, beginning at 6 pm, and ending at 6 am. Experts in spiritual warfare believe that the hours between midnight and 6 am are when principalities are most active, and this is why all-night prayer and worship times are so potent and fruitful to see breakthrough in difficult situations. The Lord Jesus had just prayed and sought the face of God through the first three watches of the night. It is no wonder that He walked on water, after this time of sweet communion with His Father! Anything is possible after soaking in the presence of God!

It would appear that the disciples of Jesus had been waiting for him a long time. Jesus had told them to go on to the other side of the lake (the Sea of Galilee) ahead of Him, while He dismissed the crowd He had been ministering to. It had been a crusade attended by well over five thousand people and Jesus had fed them all from an offering of five little loaves and two fish. When Jesus multiplied the loaves and fish, it was still the afternoon (Matthew 14:15). And when He sent His disciples and the people away it was probably not yet the first watch of the night. He may have spent about nine hours in the presence of the Father, while the disciples rowed to the other side, and then rowed back, perhaps after a meal or a nap, expecting to meet Jesus on the opposite shore. Of course, they did not see Jesus, because He was enjoying the Presence of the Father on the mountainside while they waited for him.

When it got darker and Jesus had still not appeared, they probably started to get more than a little anxious. Jesus had been away from them too long and things were not going too well for them! They were facing a sudden storm and battling the turbulent waters on the Sea of Galilee, with the wind against them. We are told that the boat was being buffeted by the waves. They were also surrounded by thick darkness - the last hours of the night always seem to be the darkest.

As they battled with the elements, we see how fear gripped the hearts and minds of these close associates of Jesus, these strong men of God. They had been waiting in the dark, maybe holding up their lamps and straining their eyes as they looked for a flicker of light on the shore. And suddenly, terror! People of the east have different superstitions about the sea and the spirits of the night. There may have been some myth that sprang into their minds as they suddenly saw a shadowy figure (Jesus) coming towards them out of the darkness. Perhaps the strong winds were playing with His robes, making Him look like He was flying. In fear they cried out that it was a 'ghost'!

We are told that Jesus quickly spoke to them aloud over the sound of the waves and the wind, identifying Himself and telling them not to be afraid, and when they heard the voice of the Lord, their hearts were set at ease.

These strong men of God were changed in a moment when they gave in to fear and anxiety. It is possible for us to be feeling strong and peaceful in the Lord, but overcome by fear in a few moments, if we allow it to take a hold of us. It happens in an instant. These men were waiting for Jesus, and suddenly, they did not even recognize Him, because their minds had opened to **fear** and let go of **faith!** This can happen to any of us if we are not mindful of it. A simple everyday situation can become a spiritual crisis, because Satan tries to attack the mind with fear. If it is allowed to come in, it can make a person crumble from the inside, an open door to the cruel attacks of the evil one. When we give in to doubt and fear we speak the devil's language. Instead of giving in to it and panicking like the disciples did, I believe God would have you:

1) **Recognize** it as a spiritual attack,
2) **Renounce** spirits of fear and anxiety. As your heart begins to beat faster, recognize the spirit of fear for what it is, and renounce it, resist it and bind it in the name of Jesus.
3) **Proclaim** your **faith** in the Almighty.
4) **Proclaim the Lordship of Jesus over your life.** *(James 4:7: "Submit yourselves, then, to God. Resist the devil, and he will flee from you.")*
5) **Speak the Word** of God out loud - for example - that God has not given you a spirit of fear, but a spirit of love, boldness and a sound mind! (2 Timothy 1:7).

As we surrender to Jesus as Lord, and wield the Sword of the Spirit (God's Word), God gives us the overcoming. As we affirm and proclaim the Word of

God constantly, it goes before us, breaking open the spiritual atmosphere, shaking off fear, and enabling us to hear the voice of God above the wind and waves once more.

6) **Know that Jesus is with you** even though you may not see or hear Him clearly through the circumstances you are in.

There may have been times in your life when you felt like you were surrounded by darkness, buffeted from every side by the waves, and tossed by the winds of your circumstances. Perhaps this is your situation today. When fear rises up and you feel like you are struggling alone, you may long to hear God's voice; you may long to see Him through the darkness of your struggle. Friend, the more you focus on your situation and confess the negative circumstances, the more the darkness may seem to press in on you; but as you embrace God's Word and change your confession, you will see its power manifested in what you are facing. You will see God fight your battle and give you the victory! It was the voice of the Master which calmed the fears of the men in the boat, and enabled them to see Him through the darkness once more. So hear the voice of the Lord today. Focus on Jesus and His Word. He is with you, He is near you. He never left you or forsook you. He is rising up from beyond the darkness to vanquish your foes and bring you the victory you seek. Know that as you begin to fight fear and stand in faith, He has begun to act on your behalf. He says "Take courage! It is I. Don't be afraid....!"

Maybe it is time for us (like the Lord Jesus) to pray through the watches of the night and see the darkness shattered around us as the Spirit of God takes control! May you see the power of the living Lord manifested in your stormy situation as you refuse to give in to fear, and believe God will work on your behalf.

Notes:

Chapter Sixteen

Just Say The Word
(Matthew 14:28-33)

"Lord if it's you," Peter replied, "tell me to come to you on the water." "Come," He said. Then Peter got down out of the boat, walked on the water and came towards Jesus. But when he saw the wind, he was afraid and, beginning to sink, cried out, "Lord, save me!" Immediately Jesus reached out His hand and caught him. "You of little faith," He said, "why did you doubt?" And when they climbed into the boat, the wind died down. Then those who were in the boat worshipped Him, saying, "Truly You are the Son of God."

There was a storm raging around the boat, and the winds were whipping the waves into it. Water was lashing upon the faces of the men as they looked out across the deep and tried to watch Jesus walking calmly over the water towards them, as the wind caught His robes and swirled around Him.

When the disciples first saw Jesus on the water, they screamed out in fear that it was a ghost! However, when Jesus reassured them and told them not to fear, Peter said *"Lord if it's You, tell me to come to you on the water."* He had walked with Jesus many years and knew by now that all things were possible with Him! The Lord Jesus just had to say the word, and the impossible became possible. When He looked at Peter through the storm, and said *"Come"*, Peter experienced a boldness he had not known a few minutes before. Watching Jesus walk on water had stirred his faith and expanded his expectations. He had hitherto probably never seen anyone do this and defy natural laws. But his heart began to consider the possibility of walking on water as He watched His teacher do it. There is no better way to learn spiritual truths than from those in authority over us. Psalm 133:2 shows us that the anointing flows from the head downwards. We partake of the anointing upon the man or woman of God in authority over us. Whatever they walk in (whether it is good or bad) will eventually flow upon the ones they lead. Peter wanted to walk on water when he saw Jesus do it. He knew he could do it if Jesus spoke the enabling Word over him. There is no greater motivation than a leader who walks in signs and wonders and has faith for the power of God to be manifested in every situation, especially when such a person speaks words of blessing and encouragement over those who serve with him or her. Peter had the perfect teacher and role model! Faith is contagious, and when you are around people of faith, you can believe for anything!

In faith Peter put his feet over the sides of the rocking boat. The howling winds were pushing against him; the churning waters were bubbling beneath his feet. But as he straightened up and let go of the side of the boat, he realized that he was not sinking through the water. The waters were bouncing under his feet, but he was walking, as though he was on dry land or standing on a water bed! And all the while, he just kept his eyes on Jesus. He had not looked at the water, or the angry winds; he had not looked up at the sky, or even his friends in the boat; he did not even look at himself and how he was doing – he was looking into the eyes of the Master. As long as he focused on Jesus, he was living a miracle – he was walking on the surface of the frothing deep, and the lashing winds and angry waters did not hinder or deter him. His heart was set on walking to Jesus. He was doing what Jesus did!

However, as he became a little more comfortable with what was happening, he stopped looking at Jesus so intensely. He took his eyes away from the King. He began to look around him. Although his spirit still focused on Jesus, his mind said 'but....'! And suddenly he was overwhelmed! The wind and the waters seemed too strong and angry for him. What he had been doing in faith suddenly dissolved as fear stepped in. He began to sink!

Friend, it is clear that if we want to do what Jesus did, and walk in all His mighty power, we have to keep our eyes on Him. Circumstances change, people come and go, but Jesus is the same yesterday, today and forever! Our source of strength and life, peace and power must be Jesus and Jesus alone. We cannot walk in the miraculous unless we walk in faith, and we cannot walk in faith unless we keep our eyes on Jesus. Fear gives birth to fear, just as faith gives birth to faith. We read in 1 Peter 5:8: *"your enemy the devil prowls around like a roaring lion looking for someone to devour"*. When we are serving and following the Lord Jesus, we cannot afford to take our eyes off Him for a moment. When we begin to listen to the voices of friends, or focus on the difficulties of our circumstances, or when we look at ourselves and begin to pat ourselves on the back, we are already beginning to sink into the waters. Maybe Peter started to think he was pretty special to be walking on the water; perhaps he started to think of how well he was doing on his own! This was a mistake – he was already sinking! The 'me' factor is the biggest danger in the equation. God in His mercy and love anoints and uses the finite frame of a human being that people may know His love and that His name may be glorified. Before too long, the person may (unknowingly) begin to believe that the gifts are theirs and that they can walk alone on the water!

Praise the Lord - we serve a God of multiple chances! When Peter realized that the formula was not working, he cried out to Jesus saying, *"Lord, save me!"* This is all it takes – to repent of our own lack of faith and 'self' focus, and cry out to Jesus. He is faithful, and He is quick to answer! Jesus reached out to Peter immediately, and held him, as He lifted him out of the water. Peter had to rise up out of the water on the strength of Jesus' faith because fear had gripped his heart once more! And Jesus rebuked him, about his shaky faith, saying *"why did you doubt"?*

When they got into the boat together, the storm died down, and the men in the boat worshipped Jesus, acknowledging that truly He was the Son of God! When Jesus steps into the boat, the storms have to submit to Him because every knee shall bow and every tongue confess that Jesus Christ is Lord (Philippians 2:10 & 11). There is no foe who can continue to stand against us when Jesus steps into our boat – demons tremble at the name of Jesus, the name above every name of every storm, sickness, bondage, or crisis. When God is for us, no one can stand against us! Jesus is calling us to trust Him, and see the mighty power of His Spirit flowing through our lives. He asks you today to:

1) Believe that all things are possible with God
2) Keep your eyes on Jesus
3) Focus on Him and not on yourself, or anyone or anything else.
4) Worship Him for the awesome Lord He is.
5) Allow Him to take over the boat – He will take you places!

Notes:

Chapter Seventeen

Waiting For the Bridegroom (Matthew 25:1-13)

"At that time the Kingdom of Heaven will be like ten virgins who took their lamps and went out to meet the bridegroom. Five of them were foolish and five were wise. The foolish ones took their lamps but did not take any oil with them. The wise, however, took oil in jars along with their lamps. The bridegroom was a long time in coming, and they all became drowsy and fell asleep.

At midnight the cry rang out: "Here's the bridegroom! Come out to meet him!" Then all the virgins woke up and trimmed their lamps. The foolish ones said to the wise, "Give us some of your oil; our lamps are going out." "No," they replied, "there may not be enough for both us and you. Instead, go to those who sell oil and buy some for yourselves". But while they were on their way to buy the oil, the bridegroom arrived. The virgins who were ready went in with him to the wedding banquet. And the door was shut. Later the others also came. "Sir! Sir"! they said, "open the door for us!" But he replied, "I tell you the truth, I don't know you." Therefore keep watch, because you do not know the day or the hour."

It was the custom of the day that prior to a marriage ceremony, the bridegroom would come to the home of the waiting bride late in the evening, attended by his friends. When those attending the bride received notice that the bridegroom was approaching, the bridesmaids would go out with lamps in their hands and lead him into the house with celebration, dancing and rejoicing.

This Scripture was a part of Jesus' teaching (Matthew chapters 24 and 25) about the end times and His return. He used a picture which was a part of the life and culture of His audience. In this parable, there were ten bridesmaids who were awaiting the arrival of the bridegroom. They all had lamps to light the bridegroom's way, but we are told that only five thought of bringing a supply of oil along. The other five used up the oil they had without any thought of a later need. When faced with a crisis, all they could think of doing was to turn to the ones who had come prepared, and ask for some of their oil. It is sad that the bridegroom arrived while they were away buying their oil, and he went into the wedding ceremony attended by the five bridesmaids who had been equipped and ready for the wait. When the other five girls came back with their replenished lamps, they were not able to get into the banquet, even though they called and cried, and asked the bridegroom to open the door for them! They simply had not been ready at the right time.

The ten virgins are symbolic of the followers of the Lord Jesus Christ and the church. Numbers always have meaning in the Word of God, and the number 'ten' represents Law, Government and Restoration. It represents a completed cycle (as in the onset of a new season). This is what the Bridegroom wants to establish when He returns to earth - the Law and Government of Heaven, and the restoration of the Kingdom. A new age! It feels like we have been waiting a long time for the return of our Bridegroom - our Lord and Savior Jesus Christ, but though He tarries, He will return, and His rule will be established over all the universe. The number 'five' is symbolic of God's grace, of atonement, the cross, and new life. This is what God desires to pour out upon those who are ready for the return of the Bridegroom; His Grace and mercy, and all the fulfillment of the blessings of the atonement and the cross of Jesus Christ - eternal fullness and life everlasting, in the presence of the King! Hallelujah!

However, the sad truth is that not all who profess the name of Jesus Christ will make it into the wedding banquet, simply because they will not be ready when the bridegroom returns. The desire of the Heavenly Father is that all His children enter in. However, while the heart of God overflows His love, grace and mercy towards His creation, there will soon be the completion of a season, (the number ten) and the close of the age, when His grace will no longer be extended. This is the time when the door will be closed behind the Bridegroom, and there will be no further opportunity to attend the wedding supper.

So how can we get ready and stay ready? By exercising the wisdom of God! It was the wise virgins who made it into the wedding banquet; they were the ones ready with their lamps still burning when they heard the bridegroom was coming, because they had a supply of oil. They too fell asleep while waiting for the bridegroom, but at least they had their jars filled with oil! Sometimes it feels like we wait forever, but the Lord is calling us to be wise while we wait. He desires that our jars be filled with oil. These are the last days of the church on earth as we know it. Jesus really **is** coming soon - all the signs point to it. He is calling us to be prepared. He seeks those whose jars are cleansed and filled with oil.

Oil is a symbol of the Holy Spirit, and God is calling us to seek the power and anointing of the Holy Spirit. He is pouring out His Spirit all over the world, like never before, and He desires that we lift up our jars and receive all the glorious goodness He has to offer us. The end time church has to be a powerful, mighty, living force - one that makes a dynamic difference in the world today; one that is walking in the power of the Spirit, with miracles, signs and wonders following! God wants the end time church to be jars filled with Holy Spirit oil. Yes, the wait is long; yes, the night around us is very dark and seems to be getting darker; yes, it feels like the bridegroom may never show up. But while we wait, the Lord would have us stay awake, alive, on fire, flowing in the oil of the Holy Spirit, and bringing His *dunamis* power to a lost and fallen world around us!

Joel prophesied (Joel 2:28-29) - *"And afterwards, I will pour out my Spirit on all people. Your sons and daughters will prophesy, your old men will dream dreams, your young men will see visions. Even on my servants, both men and women, I will pour out my Spirit in those days."* This is what is coming to pass in our time, as God prepares His people for the return of the Lord Jesus Christ. When we open our lives to the end time outpouring and allow ourselves to be filled with Holy Oil, we are stepping into that other dimension God wants us to walk in. It is one of supernatural power and Presence; one of daily signs and wonders, simply because our jars are full and continuously replenished with the oil that flows from Heaven. It is the daily latter rain, through which we can see our children prophesying in the fullness of the Holy Spirit, and the Body of Christ stepping into the realm of heavenly dreams and visions. It is a time for the ministers of the Gospel of Jesus Christ to walk in the power of miracles and divine visitations like never before, and it is all possible only when empty jars are lifted up to be filled.

There are some threads of Truth we can draw from the five wise young girls:

Firstly, the five wise virgins invested not only in the moment but also for tomorrow. They had their lamps ready and filled but they still purchased some extra oil (and maybe the jars they needed for it). They had an additional thing to carry with them as they waited for the bridegroom to come, but they did it because they knew it was important. Too many believers never stop to make an investment in their spiritual life. Because of the fast pace of life today, we may not feed on the Word, or spend time in prayer. Even in the community of the church, we may have become focused on programs and ministries, and we rush around from one thing to the other, while all the while the oil in our lamps is burning up, and in need of replenishing! We sing that these are the days of Elijah and Ezekiel, but unless the lamps are filled with oil, we will never see the power God wants to manifest through the church.

We know from the book of Revelations (1:20) that lamps are symbolic of the church. In the Old Testament, the lamp represented the presence of God in the temple; the lamp of God was never supposed to go out, and had to be replenished with fresh oil even in the dark hours of the night, so that it burned bright and strong.

God is calling us - as individuals and as the church - to understand how much we need to fill our jars and our lamps with the oil of His Word and the anointing of His Spirit. Unless we invest in our spiritual lives, we will never be able to withstand the wait victoriously. The night is dark and there are many things to hamper and hinder us and knock us down; Peter writes in 1 Peter 5:8 *"Your enemy the devil prowls around like a roaring lion looking for someone to devour...."* and in Revelations 12:12 we see that Satan is *"filled with fury, because he knows that his time is short"*. But praise God, in Daniel 11:32 we are reminded that *"the people who know their God will firmly resist him."* Hallelujah! Let us ever seek to know Him better and allow the sweet fragrance of the Holy Oil to fill us. Let us so fill our lives with His powerful Word and the anointing of the Spirit that we will be ready to dance into the wedding banquet with worship and great rejoicing, when our bridegroom comes to take us home!

Secondly, the wise virgins did not allow anyone to take away the oil that was theirs, and necessary for their wait. This may seem rather selfish, but if they had given up their oil, they may have found themselves in darkness and outside the banquet hall. There are many ways the devil tries to steal the Word and the anointing of God from our lives. He may send people to drain us and discourage us; or he may put every hindrance in our path even when we set aside time to soak in the Word and the Anointing. We may even find ourselves in unexpected situations of conflict, where we unwittingly grieve the Lord and feel distanced from His presence. The five wise girls probably felt compassion for their friends who did not have any oil; but they knew that unless they preserved what they had invested in, they would not be able to last the wait until the bridegroom came. They were not going to be denied entrance into the banquet at the eleventh hour. When the cry rang out that the bridegroom was nearly there, these five wise girls were alert, and ready to welcome the bridegroom and rejoice with him as they entered the feast that had been prepared – the wedding supper of the Lamb!

Finally, I believe the Lord would have us remember that wisdom is all about choices, which He has given us the freedom to make. We can choose to invest in the eternal things of the Spirit, or choose the temporal pleasures of this life, but some of the choices we make today can have consequences for eternity. Choose today to believe that the Bridegroom - the beautiful and glorious Prince of heaven - loves His Bride and wants her to enter the wedding banquet with Him, to enjoy sweet fellowship and communion forever. *"He has taken me to the banquet hall, and His banner over me is love"*! (Song of Songs 2:4). Jesus, the Bridegroom is calling the Bride to make herself ready (Revelations 19:7). He is passionate about His Bride. He is so in love with you!

"Let us rejoice and be glad and give Him glory! For the wedding of the Lamb has come, and His bride has made herself ready. Fine linen, bright and clean was given her to wear. (Fine linen stands for the righteous acts of the saints.) Then the angel said to me, "Write: 'Blessed are those who are invited to the wedding supper of the Lamb!' And he added, 'These are the true words of God." (Revelations 19:7-9).

Notes:

Chapter Eighteen

The Shepherd's Voice
(John 10:3-6)

"The watchman opens the gate for Him, and the sheep listen to His voice. He calls His own sheep by name and leads them out. When He has brought out all His own, He goes on ahead of them, and His sheep follow Him, because they know His voice. But they will never follow a stranger; in fact, they will run away from him because they do not recognize a stranger's voice. Jesus used this figure of speech, but they did not understand what He was telling them."

Here again Jesus used imagery which the people of the day were very familiar with. Flocks of sheep belonging to different people would often be herded together for safety in a single pen. It would be a large compound with a wall around it, to keep out wolves, thieves, and other predators. The gate would be guarded by a watchman, and when a shepherd came to take his sheep out to pasture, the watchman would open the gate for him, and let him in. The sheep of each flock recognized the voice of their shepherd, so the shepherd would call to his own sheep and lead them out one by one, out of the pen and into the open. Sheep are timid and excitable, which is why Jesus said that the sheep would never follow a stranger's voice; in fact they would run away from a stranger because his voice was alien to them and made them afraid. Once out in the open, the shepherd would walk on ahead, calling to the sheep all the time, and urging them on. The sheep were not following each other; they were not even following the physical form of the shepherd. They knew where to go, because they followed his **voice**. The terrain was rocky and sometimes dangerous; they may have been led along precarious mountain precipices; but the sheep were following the voice they trusted. They knew that if they followed the shepherd's voice, they would eventually find themselves enjoying luscious green pasture, and drinking cool spring waters! Their trust was in his voice.

Jesus was teaching the people an important spiritual lesson, but we are told that they did not understand, although it was something they really needed to hear. How much it must have grieved the Lord that although the prophets had spoken about Him through the ages, the people He came to save did not recognize Him for who He was. *"He was in the world, and though the world was made through Him, the world did not recognize Him. He came to that which was*

His own, but His own did not receive Him." (John 1: 10-11). *"The light shines in the darkness, but the darkness has not understood it..."* (John 1:5).

Many believers are in want, in sickness, in discord with themselves and those around them, because they have not followed the voice of the Shepherd. His voice has been calling them to greener pastures and clearer waters, but they have not recognized the Shepherd's voice or listened to it! It grieves the Lord when He speaks and we take no notice; or when He speaks and we do not recognize His voice. Jesus said in this passage of Scripture that **His** sheep listen to His voice. If we could train our hearts to actively and continually listen to His voice, we would always be overcomers. We would hear Him guiding us and showing us the way, and stepping in to stop us walking into situations which would be harmful or wrong for us. It would be an intrinsic part of our daily lives. We would never be defeated!

So how can we learn to walk in sensitivity to the Shepherd's voice? First, we need to recognize and distinguish the voice of evil from the voice of our Lord. **The basic test is whether the voice you hear aligns with the Word of God.** If what you hear in your heart is contrary to the Word of God, or not honoring to the Lord Jesus Christ, the Father or the Holy Spirit, know immediately that it is not the voice of the Shepherd. **The voice of the Shepherd teaches and directs you; it encourages and builds you up in your faith; it reminds you about loving and forgiving others; about humility, repentance, and the Fruit of the Spirit.** Jesus said about the Holy Spirit in John 16:8 *"When He comes, He will convict the world of guilt in regard to sin and righteousness and judgment..."* Once our spirits instinctively discern the difference, the rest is plain sailing - it becomes a way of life to see where something is coming from - whether it is of the flesh or of the Spirit - and God begins to take you to a whole new dimension! He opens up a divine realm which we can be a part of, and we can daily refine our spiritual hearing by feeding on the Word of God, and by seeking His presence through worship and prayer. This can bring us to a place where we are so open to the voice of the Holy Spirit that it is possible to hear the softest whisper amidst the biggest noise – it is a blessed state of constant communion with the Father!

It is after many years of being a follower of the Lord Jesus Christ that I truly began to be led by the voice of the Holy Spirit - it changed my life! God has filled my life with His power and His presence, and from day to day, I am learning more - to lean on Him, to be taught by Him, and to walk the path that He leads me on. This world is fraught with troubles, snares, and difficulties; but if we could be like sheep, and trust the voice of the Shepherd, and if we could be led by Him, when all the visible circumstances are telling us to change direction, we can see great victory and the power of God manifested in our daily lives. He loves us, and desires to take us to a better place! I pray that you will take time to seek the Lord and learn to discern His voice; that even in the midst of difficult circumstances, you will hear His leading and pass through rocky places to get to those green pastures and still waters. God has much in store for you! He wants to speak to you!

Notes:

Chapter Nineteen

Friend (Luke 11:5-8)

"Then He said to them, "Suppose one of you has a friend, and he goes to him at midnight and says, "Friend, lend me three loaves of bread, because a friend of mine on a journey has come to me, and I have nothing to set before him." Then the one inside answers, "Don't bother me. The door is already locked, and my children are with me in bed. I can't get up and give you anything." I tell you though he will not get up and give him the bread because he is his friend, yet because of the man's boldness, he will get up and give him as much as he needs."

In Luke 11, verse 1, the disciples of the Lord Jesus asked Him to teach them how to pray, *"just as John taught his disciples"*, and Jesus taught them the model prayer we call "the Lord's prayer". Then He gave them some deeper insights into our basis for prayer.

Jesus used the illustration of a person going to a friend's house for help at a very inconvenient time. The friend was not inclined to help him because of the lateness of the hour, but cooperated in the end. Think about this scenario for a moment, putting yourself in the shoes of either person! Most of us would be happy to help others even at some inconvenience to ourselves, but many of us would think twice before approaching someone else for help, unless we had a close relationship with them. It could be because we hesitate to impose upon others and put them to effort or inconvenience; it could also be because it is not easy to humble ourselves and become indebted to another! However, the person in this passage had no such inhibitions. It was late at night, and not the usual time for knocking on another person's door, but he still approached the home of his friend and called out loudly to him. He was determined to wake him up! He was determined not to go away empty handed.

This whole exchange was on the basis of the **relationship** there was between the two people. The **boldness** to ask, as well as the honest answer was because of the **close friendship**. When the first man (let's call him Tim) approached the home of the other man (John) for help, Tim knew that because of the lateness of the hour, John would be asleep in bed. In the hospitable Eastern culture of the time, a person's front door would always be open because guests were always welcome and just showed up at your door. If the front door and windows were shut, then it was obvious that it was not a time for visitors. John's door and windows were probably shut and barred for security because it was the end of the day. Not only was he asleep, but his family were tucked up in bed with him. Any parent knows that once small children are asleep, it is better not to disturb them! Once they wake up, it is not easy to get them back to sleep again. John did not want a bunch of tired, irritable children, wide awake and crying because their sleep was disturbed. That would mean a sleepless night for the whole household! So when Tim started knocking on his door and calling out his name loudly, asking for some bread for his unexpected guest, John probably wished he had a shotgun by his side! It is clear to see that there was a very close friendship, and a level of familiarity between the two people. This is why Tim went to John's house in the first place. This is also why John felt free to reply so rudely - he was virtually saying 'get lost buddy - you've got to be joking'! He said to Tim *"I can't get up and give you anything at this time"*. But as Tim persisted, continuing to knock and demand, he finally got out of bed and gave him everything he asked for.

There are some threads of truth we can take from this passage and apply to our own prayer lives:

1) Jesus spoke about the man's 'boldness'. It came from the close friendship they shared. They were each completely comfortable to speak their hearts to the other, and to be themselves with each other. They enjoyed a level of closeness and intimacy, and Tim approached John believing that John would help him out in the end. He also asked without a fear of being rebuffed.

We can see that what we may hesitate to do with our human friends, we can feel free to do with God. What people may consider an imposition, God never will. As a father with His children, our Abba God is delighted when we recognize our identity in Christ and our authority as His blood bought children. He wants us to come **boldly** to His presence in the name of His Son Jesus and freely bring our requests before Him. Unlike Tim and John, remember He is the One who never slumbers or sleeps (Psalm 121:4)! We can approach Him any time of day or night.

2) Persistence and perseverance made a difference. Tim did not give up, even though at first he did not get the answer he came for. Romans 2:7 shows us that persistence in our spiritual life brings great rewards. Being a disciple of the Lord Jesus Christ is all about perseverance. James 1:12 says *"Blessed is the man who perseveres..."* To see growth and anointing in our spiritual walk and in our prayer life, we have to press on, and continuously persevere in the face of hindrance and adversity. Tim kept on knocking and asking because he knew his friend so well. He knew his heart, and that he would finally help him out, despite the lateness of the hour. **He also knew that John had a supply of bread in his house!** He would not have come to him if he thought John did not have the means to help him at that time of the night.

3) Tim's request was for someone else. His intercession was on behalf of a friend. This is the heart of our Lord and Savior, Jesus Christ. He is seated at the right hand of the Father, interceding on our behalf even now. When we pray for others, we speak His language of love. He sees the selflessness, and the love which motivates the petitioner. It is His will and desire that we pray for others, even as He prayed for us in the book of John Chapter 17, and as He prays for us eternally.

4) He received as much as he needed. Exceedingly abundantly more than we could ever ask or imagine! This is how God answers His children who boldly come to Him, believing that He desires to bless them! He looks for those who have faith to ask, and faith enough to believe they will receive.

Finally, our Savior is the *'friend who sticks closer than a brother'* (Proverbs 18:24). We know that He truly desires to be friends with us because we see from the Word that this is how He regarded the people He chose and called to be His own. In Exodus 33:11 we are told that He spoke with Moses as a man speaks with his "friend". Abraham too was described as God's "friend" (2 Chronicles 20:7, James 2:23, Isaiah 41:8). In John 15:13 Jesus said that He was laying down His life for His 'friends', and that we are His "friends" if we do what He commands (John 15:14). He is ours and we are His. He is our Lord and King, our Father and Savior, but we are also friends!

Precious friend of Jesus, I pray that your prayer life will be transformed from this day onwards. I pray that you will see the blessed relationship you have with the Father, and the love there is between you and Him! **Be bold and persistent**. Remember that there may be many reasons why you have not seen an answer to your heart's cry, hindrances which God wants to overturn for you. Stay with it, persist, seek the direction of the Holy Spirit as you pray, and see God work wonders in your life and in the lives of those you are praying for. We all need friends in high places, and you have a powerful friend!

Notes:

Chapter Twenty

Staying On Track
(Matthew 16:21-23)

"From that time on Jesus began to explain to His disciples that He must go to Jerusalem and suffer many things at the hands of the elders, chief priests and teachers of the law, and that He must be killed, and on the third day be raised to life. Peter took him aside and began to rebuke Him. "Never, Lord!" he said. "This shall never happen to you!" Jesus turned and said to Peter, "Get behind me, Satan! You are a stumbling block to me; you do not have in mind the things of God, but the things of men".

This message is from the heart of God for all the precious people who need to focus on the Lord and overcome the hindrances of the evil one.

The Lord Jesus had no doubts about what He had been sent to do on earth. From the beginning of His ministry, He focused completely on submitting to the will of the Father, and walking towards the final mission - the supreme sacrifice of Himself - in order that God's divine plan of salvation would be fulfilled. In the passage of Scripture just prior to this one (Matthew 16:13-20), Peter had the revelation of who Jesus really was. Suddenly he saw beyond the prophet, teacher and rabbi. In a flash, he saw with the eyes of Heaven and understood the divinity of Jesus, and His redemptive power. He proclaimed Him as the Christ, and the Son of the living God. This was a spiritual awakening!

Jesus saw that His disciples were maturing spiritually, and understanding things of the supernatural realm, and He began to explain to them some of the things that would happen to Him in the days to come - His arrest and suffering at the hands of the Jews, and how He would be killed and later, raised to life. Jesus knew what He had to do to complete His mission. He was so focused on obeying the will of the Father that many times in the Gospels we see how He spoke about 'finishing' the work the Father sent Him to do. Just before his Spirit left His body as He hung on the cross, He said *'It is finished'!* Jesus had no intention of leaving anything undone that He came to do, however painful or difficult.

In the same way, God has given most of us a mission on this earth. He has assigned each of us a task to fulfill and wants us to see it through. In offices, schools and colleges, in homes, hospitals and out in the streets, there is work to be done; there are lives to be touched. When we are at the end of this earthly life, God wants us to be able to say (like Jesus) that we finished the race and completed our mission. This is something possible for all of us, whatever the assignment God has given us, so long as we learn from Jesus, and follow His example!

When we take a step forward in the ministry or in our relationship with God, our enemy the devil does not sit back and give up what used to be a part of his kingdom of darkness. It is never an easy fight, but if we walk in the wisdom and understanding of God, and in the power of His Spirit, we cannot be beaten down. God enables us to always complete the task and go the last mile. He gives us the victory. Sometimes the most glorious successes are the ones that were really fought for!

Jesus always discerned the difference between flesh and Spirit. Ephesians 6:12 tells us that *"our battle is not against flesh and blood but against the rulers, against the authorities, against the powers of this dark world and against the spiritual forces of evil in the heavenly realms"*. In Matthew 16:17, when Peter declared that Jesus was the Christ and the Son of God, Jesus said to him that this had not been revealed to him by flesh and blood but by God Himself! Now, not long after, Jesus saw that Peter was speaking through a wrong spirit. He loved Jesus and did not want to see him suffer, and he surely never consciously intended to be a source of discouragement to Jesus. But when he began to refute the words that Jesus spoke, and say that they would never come to pass, Jesus saw where this was coming from!

Jesus expected trouble from the Pharisees and the Jewish leaders; He knew that they would initiate and carry through His persecution and crucifixion. We too realize we have an enemy, and we probably would not be too surprised if we found an ugly person with an evil face, horns and a pitchfork waiting around the corner to trip us up! This is why the devil hardly ever hits at us directly. He manipulates those around us - in our fellowship groups and churches, in our homes and places of work. He sometimes uses even the family and friends we love and listen to, who may be quite unaware of what is happening. Be like Jesus. Be discerning!

When you know without a doubt that God has called you to take a step for Him, be aware that discouragement could come against you through the opinions and advice of those you care about. Of course these dear people are motivated by their love for you, but Satan uses this to place a stumbling block in your path. We may not want to speak to them as Jesus spoke to Peter (!), but as we continue to relate to them in love, we can quietly take authority over the spirits working behind them, and bind every spirit of hindrance and discouragement in Jesus' name. You can be sure that words that cause a sense of heaviness and a feeling of discouragement in your heart are not from the Lord. Peter was not focusing on the fact that although Jesus spoke about his crucifixion, he also mentioned his resurrection. It seems like all he could see was the pain of the cross. He did not want to see the One he loved suffer at the hands of the Jews, and the devil used this to try to draw Jesus away from the plan of God. Satan attempts to use the relationships and emotional attachments we have, to bring pressure upon us to cave in and choose the easy way rather than the difficult path; this is sometimes a path of pain and inconvenience, which is really the path to victory, the cross, and the resurrection! People often only focus on the seeming inconveniences or difficulties of obeying our Father and following Jesus, and try to make us do the same. But as Jesus said to Peter, when we focus on the things of God and not on the things of the world and the flesh, we are able to develop the discernment we need to be the overcomers God wants us to be. We will not be hindered in our God ordained walk; neither will we be used as a stumbling block in the life of another.

There are four keys we could remember as we press on, resist every discouraging dart and stay on the road to victory, upon which we have been called to walk:

1) Remember our battle is not with flesh and blood (Ephesians 6:12).
2) Be aware that you are in a battle and be alert always (1 Peter 5:8).
3) Stand firm and keep doing what God called you to do (Ephesians 6:13 & 14).
4) Cultivate a walk of self control and holiness (1 Peter 5:8, 1 Peter 2:9) so that the devil gets no foothold.

Above all, remember that you are not fighting alone and that the Lord is always with you. The One who is in us is greater than the one who is in the world! (1 John 4:4). God and you are a mighty army. 1 John 3:8 says that *"the reason the Son of God appeared was to destroy the devil's work"*. No foe can prevail against you if you have God on your side. When He calls you to be a part of His plan, He empowers you to overcome every enemy attack!

I declare over you today the words of the prophet Isaiah (54:17), that *"no weapon formed against you will prosper and every tongue that rises up against you will be silenced"*, in the mighty name of Jesus Christ our Lord and victorious Conqueror! May God fill you with His power to stay on track, to overcome, and to finish the race!

Notes:

Chapter Twenty One

Carrying the Cross (Matthew 16:24-27)

"Then Jesus said to His disciples, "If anyone would come after me, he must deny himself and take up his cross and follow me. For whoever wants to save his life will lose it, but whoever loses his life for me will find it. What good will it be for a man if he gains the whole world, yet forfeits his soul? Or what can a man give in exchange for his soul? For the Son of Man is going to come in His Father's glory with His angels, and then He will reward each person according to what he has done."

The last chapter was about discerning between flesh and spirit in order to stay on track. As we continue to look at Matthew 16, there is further insight we can receive about how the Lord Jesus stood His ground, and finished His assignment here on earth.

When Peter began to tell Jesus that the cross and its path of pain would never happen to Him, (Matthew 16:23) Jesus rebuked Peter and addressed the spirit behind his words. Then He said to Peter: *"You are a stumbling block to me; you do not have in mind the things of God, but the things of men"*. He was telling Peter that his heart and mind were preoccupied with the temporal things of the flesh, rather than the divine purposes of God. We can stumble ourselves and hinder God's plan for us, when our focus is on the values and the mindsets of the world. We may be unwittingly submitting ourselves to all the manipulation and influences of the spirit of the world. Jesus tells us how to overcome this, and go on to higher ground in our walk with Him. He tells us to take up the cross and follow in His footsteps! This sounds very simple and basic, but serious disciples of the Lord Jesus know this is not an easy path. It means standing for everything the Lord Jesus stood for. Although we associate the cross with pain, the cross is the way to resurrection power and life. Paul wrote in 1 Corinthians 1:18 *"....the message of the cross is foolishness to those who are perishing, but to us who are being saved it is the power of God."*

So what did Jesus really mean when He told His disciples to carry their cross and follow Him?

The cross means self-denial. It means laying down our own desires and will, and surrendering to those of the Father. It means desiring to please Him whatever the cost, even when we may receive the ridicule or rejection of people. It means taking the steps that are ordained by the Lord and staying on the path He leads us on, even when the going gets tough and the tough get going! Nobody who is really following Jesus walks without a cross. The cross is not some trial, sickness or hardship we suffer in the flesh. Rather, it is the spiritual, mental and physical persecutions and pressures that may come simply because we choose to tread a no-compromise path in the footsteps of Jesus.

The cross is the path of prayer. The Lord Jesus was always in communication with the Father, even up to the last moments on the cross, when He cried out 'It is finished' He was telling His Dad 'I did it'! There is no way we can continue on the path God has called us to walk, and finish the assignments He has given us unless we are in constant communication with God through the Holy Spirit. This is our source of life and strength. This is how we may receive the leading and guidance of God to walk in His will. It is how we experience the supernatural discernment and power we need to overcome the hindrances and attacks of the enemy, and finish the race victoriously. In the relentless pace of life today, it is sometimes a battle to make room for prayer. Where we cannot find large spaces of time to pray, the best alternative is to fit in little pockets of ten or fifteen minutes at a time, to seek God, worship Him and listen to His Word. It is possible to experience the refreshing anointing of God in the car, the office, or a quiet corner of a school playground. This way we can stay in tune with His voice, and open to receive His leading.

The cross is the path of fasting. The Lord Jesus regularly fasted. This strengthens us spiritually and gives us power to overcome the flesh and the attacks of the evil one. It helps us to focus and fill ourselves with the *'things of God'* (Matthew 16:23). There are many different kinds of fasts, and you need to choose the one that best suits your body and lifestyle. When fasting, it is powerful to feed yourself with big meals of the Word of God. This grows your spirit and makes it strong to stay on track!

Be willing to lose yourself to gain Jesus and be like Him. Jesus said here that when we try to preserve our own identity, status, rights, ambitions etc, we may gain the recognition and rewards of the world, but we may lose the real glory we could know in Him. (See Matthew 5:11& 12, Matthew 6:6, and Matthew 6:18). On the other hand, when we commit to die to our own plans, and to our desires for human acceptance and acclaim, and when we lose our life and our self focus to follow Jesus, we gain real and eternal rewards and the acknowledgement of Heaven! There is no earthly treasure, no fame that could ever compare to the spiritual riches of doing the will of the Father. Jesus said that we have lost everything if we gain the rewards of the world at the cost of Heaven's rich rewards! To be in the right place with God is the most valuable treasure we could have, and it is all for an eternal purpose. This is good news! Jesus is coming back one day soon, not as a helpless little baby, but as the triumphant and glorious King and Lord, with thousands of the Heavenly Host descending the skies with Him. And He will reward His disciples who faithfully stayed the course, carried the cross, and walked the narrow path He called them to! This is our hope and our joy! This is what we live for and look towards. We are His forever!

I pray that you will be strengthened and encouraged, as you read this message, to stay on the path you have been called to walk, and to carry the cross to the finish. You can do all things through Christ who strengthens you!

Notes:

Chapter Twenty Two

Dare to be a Disciple
(Matthew 8:16-22)

"When evening came, many who were demon-possessed were brought to Him, and He drove out the spirits with a word and healed all the sick. This was to fulfill what was spoken through the Prophet Isaiah: "He took up our infirmities and carried our diseases."

When Jesus saw the crowd around Him, He gave orders to cross to the other side of the lake. Then a teacher of the law came to Him and said, "Teacher, I will follow You wherever You go." Jesus replied, "Foxes have holes and birds of the air have nests, but the Son of Man has nowhere to lay His head." Another disciple said to Him, "Lord, first let me go and bury my father." But Jesus told him, "Follow me, and let the dead bury their own dead."

This chapter is about what it takes to be a real disciple of the Lord Jesus. The many people who claim the name of Jesus can be divided into three groups: -

1) **Friends of Jesus** (Those who have positive feelings for the Lord Jesus and even accept some of His teachings).

2) **Followers of Jesus** (Those who receive His Word into their lives and seek to walk in it where possible).

3) **Disciples of Jesus** - The Websters' Dictionary defines a disciple as *"someone who accepts and assists in spreading the doctrines of another; a convinced adherent of a school or individual"*. Also: *"an active adherent of a movement or philosophy"*. An 'adherent' is defined as a person who 'adheres', (as through a contract), and the word 'adhere' may be translated as: "connected", "holding fast" or "sticking as if by gluing, suction, grasping, or fusing"!

So a disciple of Jesus can be described as someone who actively lives the Christian life and passes on the Good News constantly, through a purposeful lifestyle of witness. A disciple is one who has entered into a contract and covenant with the Lord Jesus Christ, through the partaking of His Blood, and who sticks to Him through thick and thin, unswayed by circumstances that arise, however difficult they may be.

In the first few verses of this passage of Scripture, we see what it means to be a true disciple and do the things that Jesus did - He delivered the demon possessed **with a word**, and healed **all** the sick. The life of true discipleship is one of walking above the storms of life, and living in the dimensions of supernatural power. But how do we get there? Read on!

Firstly, Jesus had been ministering to the sick and the oppressed, and He was in the midst of hundreds of people milling around Him, seeking one more touch and one more taste of His Glory! He then *"gave orders to cross to the other side of the lake"*. There were hundreds and thousands of "friends" of Jesus, and also many "followers" around Him, but **to become a disciple, we have to be ready to cross over to the other side.** Many believe they are disciples but they have not crossed over. God is looking for those who will get off the fence, turn their backs on every sin and compromise, and take a stand to live a life that is transparent, free and powerfully filled with the fruitfulness of the Blessed Holy Spirit. Of course, we are all 'work in progress', and God continues to deal with us after we get to the other side! But until we take a step away from the 'old things' and cross over to the 'other side' we will never see true "Jesus Power" manifesting in and through our lives. God wants to deal with us in ever greater degrees, even in our innermost thoughts and feelings. He wants to change mindsets and worldviews; He wants us to shed lifetime, or generational, thought patterns and habits. This may be painful, but releases amazing power and anointing we may never otherwise see. In these last days, when God is calling the Bride to get ready for the return of the Bridegroom, we cannot afford to sit on the fence and long to be partakers of the latter rain and the end time outpouring that is coming. We have to cross over to the other side, where it is all happening!

Secondly, when the teacher of the law said that he would follow Jesus wherever He went, Jesus replied that He had nowhere to lay His head. (This verse is not about Jesus being poor – He was not!) It is about following Jesus at any cost. The teachers of the law (the scribes) and the Pharisees persecuted and crucified Jesus, because they could not let go of the burden of the law and open their hearts to Him. Jesus wanted this man to understand that following Him and being His disciple could never be a superficial thing. It could never be compared to following and obeying the law, which can be done through schooling the mind and disciplining the body. **Being a disciple of Jesus is a matter of the heart.** It means going where He goes because we love Him and long to be where He is. It means doing what He does, however great the cost. Jesus was pointing out to this man that while he had just seen some incredible miracles and blessings poured out, there was a price to pay. We may lose some of the things we take for granted, like the love and acceptance of our peers, because we choose to cross over to the other side. But we cross over **with Him**, because we are in love - with the beautiful and precious One who is so in love with each of us that He gave His very life! We do not seek Jesus because of anything He could give us or do for us (even if we had nowhere to lay our heads!). We seek Him because He is so incredibly precious and worthy of our love and commitment.

Thirdly, when a man asked if he could first go and bury his father, Jesus told him to come after Him and let the dead bury their own dead. He was saying that **Discipleship is a matter of the Spirit.** A true disciple abandons all dead works, and legalistic practices of the flesh, and opens himself/herself to the things of the Spirit. A disciple lives in obedience to the Holy Spirit. Discipleship is about looking forward and not looking back! This man was looking back at something that was finished and gone, when there was limitless power and potential opening up before him in connecting to that *kairos* moment and going to the other side with Jesus. Sometimes we focus on the 'dead' failures or hurts, or even the traditions and practices of the past, when there is so much that is alive and taking shape before us. There may also be occasions when the Lord opens up new doors before us, which we hesitate to walk through because we are afraid of the unknown. What you have may be familiar and comfortable, but if Jesus is calling you to something else, be a disciple, stop looking back to where you were, and step up to where He is taking you. The past is over and dead. The future is filled with promise and divine potential. As you step forward in faith, you will see the fulfillment of things that were once prophesied for your life! God has glorious plans to prosper you in all you do. He has a blessed future for you!

Friend, let the Word of God challenge you today! Rise up and fly high. Fly free! Dare to be a real disciple of the King of Kings and walk in the abundant blessing and power He has for you!

Notes:

Chapter Twenty Three

Abiding In the Vine
(John 15:1-8)

*"I am the true Vine, and my Father is the Gardener.
He cuts off every branch in me that bears no fruit,
while every branch that does bear fruit He prunes
so that it will be even more fruitful. You are already
clean because of the word I have spoken to you.
Remain in me, and I will remain in you. No branch
can bear fruit by itself; it must remain in the vine.
Neither can you bear fruit unless you remain in
me.*

*I am the Vine; you are the branches. If a man
remains in me and I in him, he will bear much
fruit; apart from me you can do nothing. If anyone
does not remain in me, he is like a branch that is
thrown away and withers; such branches are picked
up, thrown into the fire and burned. If you remain
in me and my words remain in you, ask whatever*

you wish and it will be given to you. This is to my Father's glory, that you bear much fruit, showing yourselves to be my disciples."

On the night before His crucifixion, the Lord Jesus spent time with His disciples, as He taught them Kingdom Keys and prepared them for His return to Heaven. He used another picture which was typical to the culture and the place, of the vine and the gardener or vinedresser.

Israel was identified as God's vine in the Old Testament. God was the "Gardener", who took care of the Vine – His people, cutting off branches that were not bearing fruit, and generally providing all the conditions necessary for the vine to grow and prosper. The Old Testament has many prophetic messages in which God refers to Israel as a vine. The vine became so much a symbol of Israel that it appeared on coins minted during the Maccabean period, which was between the Old and New Testaments. According to historians, during the time of Jesus, Herod's Temple had a huge vine on it overlaid with gold which some have estimated was worth about $12,000,000. Israel had always been God's vine, but a new vine was established when the old one became unproductive.

In the same way, there are two kinds of branches which Jesus refers to – those that do not bear fruit and those that do. Judas had just left the room, and Jesus was in the room with the eleven 'true' disciples – the ones that would 'remain' in Him. The twelfth branch had already been severed from the tree. Jesus explained to His disciples that if they were to experience the blessings of the New Covenant, they had to be in union with Him, and living to please Him; they had to draw nourishment and strength from their relationship with Him and Him **alone**. Salvation had made them 'clean' but fruitfulness could only come by clinging to Jesus, and **remaining** in Him.

The Lord Jesus seeks to see fruitfulness in our lives, not only in terms of signs and wonders and good works in His Kingdom, but also in the manifestations of the fruit of the Spirit (Galatians 6), humility, the love walk, and life transformation as we respond to the hand of the Master Gardener.

Disciples of the Lord Jesus may attach themselves to many different 'vines'. We need to honestly assess our lives with the help of the Holy Spirit, and see what we really draw our sense of worth from, and what we invest our hearts in. What really gives us a sense of identity and affirmation? It could be some educational label, or the possession of an asset; it could be a family name or college we attended; it could be the organizations we work for, or the people we associate with; it could even be a church or Christian ministry. Whatever we draw our value from, it cannot ever result in the kind of fruit Jesus referred to, unless we have given the first place to the True Vine – our Lord and Savior Jesus Christ, and walk with Him and in Him from day to day.

Jesus spoke about the fruitless branches as the ones that did not stay connected to the vine. These were compared to severed branches, which withered away useless, until they were thrown away and burned up. These are the disciples who attached themselves to the wrong vine; or who thought they could bear fruit through their own labor and striving.

Let us focus on the fruitful branches which are tended by the Master Gardener:

The fruitful branches are the ones that 'abide' in the True vine. This means walking each day in a heart to heart, spirit to Spirit connection with the Lord Jesus Christ. These are the disciples who went further than praying a prayer for salvation. They are the ones who live each day not for themselves but for the glory and honor of the King of kings. They are the ones who seek the presence of the Lord each day and feed on His Word, that His words may *"remain"* in them. These are the disciples to whom the Lord Jesus made a powerful promise: ***"If you remain in me and my words remain in you, ask whatever you wish, and it will be given to you."***

1) **Pruning is a painful process for the vine.** It may appear to the observer as though the gardener hacks off branches randomly, because the tree may look so bare and lifeless afterwards. But this results in a healthier tree which flourishes incrementally, bearing leaves, flowers and fruit, and one from which many can receive food and drink. If the branch has to feel the pain of the knife anyway, I would rather be pruned than cut away from the Tree! I would rather be cor-

rected and disciplined by my heavenly Father than left to wither and fall away.

2) **There is a purpose for the pruning** – it brings greater fruitfulness and deeper dependence on the Vine. It results in fruit which the Father delights in. It leads to the development of maturity and discernment. It increases our faith in God.

3) Salvation is wonderful and God's precious gift. It is the result of having an encounter with the Living Lord and experiencing His forgiveness; **but fruitfulness is a result of clinging to the Vine** and staying there.

4) **If we hold on to the Vine, the Vine holds on to us.** (*"Draw near to God and He will draw near to you"* – James 4:8.) Fruitfulness is the natural manifestation of the life and nourishment which flow into the branches from the Vine. Jesus reminds us that apart from the Vine we can do nothing. Peace, joy, health, healing, signs and wonders all flow when our source is the Vine.

5) **The Father's name is glorified,** when our lives bear the fruit He seeks. This should be our heart's desire – to bring glory and honor to the name of the King.

Friend, the Lord Jesus is talking about us staying in relationship with Him. He is talking about a two-way street; about constant communication, and cooperation with the blessed Holy Spirit. He is talking about being true branches, growing out of the True vine. This is the only way to fruitfulness in Jesus.

I pray that you will put Jesus first and seek Him through worship and His Word, and that you will see the precious blessedness which flows to bear fruit in every area of your life. Remember the promise He has given us - the secret to answered prayer: *"If you remain in me and my words remain in you, ask whatever you wish, and it will be given to you."* Amen!

Notes:

Chapter Twenty Four

To My Bride…
(Revelations 2:1-7)

"To the angel of the church in Ephesus write: These are the words of Him who holds the seven stars in His right hand and walks among the seven golden lamp stands: I know your deeds, your hard work and your perseverance. I know that you cannot tolerate wicked men, that you have tested those who claim to be apostles but are not, and have found them false. You have persevered and have endured hardships for my name, and have not grown weary.

Yet I hold this against you: You have forsaken your first love. Remember the height from which you have fallen! Repent and do the things you did at first. If you do not repent, I will come to you and remove your lampstand from its place. But you have this in your favor: You hate the practices of Nicolaitans, which I also hate.

He who has an ear, let him hear what the Spirit says to the churches. To him who overcomes, I will give the right to eat from the tree of life, which is in the paradise of God."

This powerful message to the church of God is a part of the revelation given to the Apostle John while he was a prisoner on the island of Patmos. Transported to Heaven in visions, John saw the Lord Jesus, and the end time events which will bring this age to a close. There is *dunamis* power within the book of Revelations, because in verse 3 of chapter 1, it says *"Blessed is the one who reads the words of this prophecy, **and** blessed are those who hear it and take to heart what is written in it, because the time is near"*. There is a double blessing within this book!

John wrote that while he was praying and in the Spirit, he heard the voice of God telling him to write down the messages he would receive for the seven churches mentioned. (Ephesus, Smyrna, Pergamum, Thyatira, Sardis, Philadelphia and Laodicea). John saw the Lord Jesus standing among seven golden lamp stands (the seven churches), awesome and radiant with Glory, with eyes like blazing fire and feet like bronze glowing in a furnace. He held seven stars in His hand and out of His mouth was a sharp, double edged sword, the Word of God (Revelations 1:12-16). The seven stars were the seven pastors/ leaders of the seven churches. It is powerful to know that God deals with each part of His Body, the church, individually; that He sees the needs, the challenges, the strengths and weaknesses, and that it is His desire that we walk in a spirit of victory. He desires that we grow in the power of the Holy Spirit, to reach our fullest potential in Him, so that His name may be glorified upon the earth. It is also a blessing to know that the Lord is in our midst - **'among'** the churches (the lamp stands - 1:13), and that His right hand is upon those He has called (Revelations 1:16). Satan cannot destroy what God has set His hand to build, and come what may, the will of God shall be fulfilled. His Spirit is moving in the midst of His Bride. He will turn around what needs to be turned around; He will break what needs to be broken; He will shake what has to shake! Hallelujah!

In this message to the church in Ephesus, the Lord commends many of their strengths. Through what He spoke to the people of the Ephesian church, the Lord Jesus Christ is telling us today that He sees the commitment of His people. He sees the hard work, the faithfulness, the perseverance in times of attack and adversity; He sees the hunger for righteousness among many, and the fierce, no-compromise desire for holiness. He sees the maturity of discernment and the wisdom to recognize truth from falsehood. He sees that there are many who will not tolerate false doctrines and deception (the practices of the Nicolaitans). He sees the single-hearted devotion, and the tenacity to hang on to faith and the Word even in the face of painful persecution in these last days. The Lord is commending His faithful ones today - He sees your service and dedication and blesses you for it! You are precious in His sight!

Yet....! Our Lord loves, values and appreciates all the times we have stayed close to Him and walked in His ways and in His work, but He says **'yet'**....! There is something He is asking of us His children, whom He loves and cherishes enough to give His very life for. He longs for the first passion of the love we used to offer Him. He is seeking that we return to those first sweet days of hungering for Him and seeking His presence; the days when we would wake up in the night and call His name as a tender caress; those times when we turned down the human diversions and demands on our time, just to wait a while with Him! Jesus our Bridegroom is calling us back to those first sweet honeymoon moments, when He was the thought which was always on our minds. He sees the difference in our attitude to Him now and He says "repent - remember the height from which you have fallen! Do the things you did at first." Jesus, our Lover; Jesus the Husband and Bridegroom - He is longing for a renewal of the covenant of love. Yes, He sees how we faithfully fulfill our commitments; and He sees that we have not fallen into sin or given the first place to any other god. But that is not all He looks for from us. The Lord Jesus says that if we do not make right our relationship with Him, He will 'remove the lamp stand from its place'. This means that He will take His presence from us (as individuals or as a group), until it is just like any other place, or any other person, who never knew the presence of God in their lives. What a fearful, terrible tragedy - to once know the power, presence and manifestation of God and then not have Him any more. It is in fact the sad reality for many individuals and ministries, that the presence of the Lord has left them and they are not even aware of it! They simply continue with business as usual.

King David cried out to God in Psalm 51 verse 11, saying: *"Do not cast me from your presence or take your Holy Spirit from me..."* God continues to manifest His presence where people are hungry and thirsty for Him. He comes where His Spirit is wanted and given freedom to move and flow as He wills. But as the hunger gets less, so does His presence, until little by little, our worship and our relationship become a ritual and a tradition; a habitual thing, devoid of fire, empty of passion. It becomes a flickering candle where once there was a roaring flame, and all that is left is the good works that we continue to offer faithfully to our God. It happens so subtly, so gradually, that we may not even realize that there is anything amiss, and how far we have fallen, until the Lord points it out to us as He did to the Ephesian believers.

In this passage of Scripture, the Lord Jesus says: *"He who has an ear, let him hear what the Spirit says to the churches. To him who overcomes, I will give the right to eat from the tree of life, which is in the paradise of God."* He is speaking to all those who are receptive to His voice and desire the moving of His Spirit in their lives and hearts; the Lord is telling us that there is a great reward in store when we fall in love with Jesus all over again - it is a special place in Heaven - eternal life and glory in the presence of our God. His heart's desire is that His bride will seek

Him and run into His arms through worship; that His bride will love Him with a passion, a desire, and a longing, and without any reservations; He wants His bride to be faithful in holiness, and love Him and Him alone - He will share that first place with no one else!

Friend, let us listen to what the Spirit is telling us today; God is speaking to you and me. He is telling us that even our Kingdom service can get in the way of our heart relationship with Him. He wants to be our priority. He wants us to be so in love with Him that we will be willing to lay everything down, just to get closer to Him and have some more of His precious presence in our lives!

I pray that you will backtrack to the day you first fell in love with Jesus; may He so touch you through His Word today that you will fall on your knees and make a fresh covenant with Him - a covenant of love - to love Him, honor Him and obey Him, for ever and ever, for the glory of His name! Amen!

Notes:

Chapter Twenty Five

To My Bride -
2 (Revelations 3:7-13)

"To the angel of the church in Philadelphia write: These are the words of Him who is holy and true, who holds the key of David. What He opens no one can shut, and what He shuts no one can open. I know your deeds. See, I have placed before you an open door that no one can shut. I know that you have little strength, yet you have kept my Word and have not denied my name. I will make those who are of the synagogue of Satan, who claim to be Jews though they are not, but are liars - I will make them come and fall down at your feet and acknowledge that I have loved you. Since you have kept my command to endure patiently, I will also keep you from the hour of trial that is going to come upon the whole world to test those who live on the earth.

I am coming soon. Hold on to what you have, so that no one will take your crown. Him who over-comes I will make a pillar in the temple of my God. Never again will he leave it. I will write on him the name of my God and the name of the city of my God, the new Jerusalem, which is coming down out of heaven from my God; and I will also write on him my new name. He who has an ear, let him hear what the Spirit says to the churches."

This is another of the seven messages given to the Apostle John for the seven churches. It is a message for us today, from Him who is Holy and True - our Lord and Savior Jesus Christ, who gave His life that we might live; the Faithful One, who has promised He will never leave us.

These are uncertain times economically and spiritually. The world over, there is hardly anyone who has not been affected by the turbulence in the world economy, and the spiritual undercurrents, touching lives and spreading a fear and anxiety about the future. But the Lord seeks to encourage and strengthen us in Him today. He is the Eternal and Everlasting Lord who never changes. He is the beginning and the end. His promises that were true yesterday are the same today. He desires that we begin to focus not on the circumstances around us, but beyond - His Love, His Word, His faithfulness to us in adversity. He wants us to see the eternal nature of our relationship with Him. Above and beyond any earthly circumstance, He is Lord! He holds the 'key of David'. The key signifies rulership, ownership, power and authority;

we know from the Old Testament that God made a covenant with King David, that his descendants would always be the leaders of the land. The name David means 'beloved', and the Lord is reminding us here that we - His beloved - were chosen to rule and reign with Him in heavenly places. Jesus said to His disciples in Matthew 28:18 that all authority in heaven and on earth have been given to Him. This is the same authority He delegates to us His chosen, to be the victors, to always be the head and not the tail! (Luke 9:1). He has given us a crown which symbolizes leadership, dominion and rule (*"Hold on to what you have so that no one will take your crown."*).

The Lord is assuring us here that no one can take away the opportunities He has given us, and the favor He has placed upon us. The doors He has opened can never be shut. Things may become quite dire around us, but we cannot lose what God has given us unless we decide to let it go. (The Lord Jesus said to the Philadelphian church: *"hold on to what you have"*). This applies to every gift we have received from God - whether spiritual, material, or physical. Value it, and enjoy what you have with thankfulness. Stop anticipating its loss, and instead, sow it into the life of another! The Lord knows the hearts of His children. He knows the ones who seek to please Him. He knows those who are His, despite the defeats and difficulties along the way. In fact, He promises in this passage of Scripture that His protection and covering will be upon us in these last days when the difficulties (the hour of trial) will increase and affect people across the whole world. He even says that those 'disciples' who maligned and misunderstood you will have to back down and acknowledge that God is truly working in and through your life; they will have to acknowledge God's love and anointing upon you!

These promises are wonderfully encouraging, but how do we receive them? In this passage, the Lord Jesus speaks twice about faithfulness to His Word: *"...I know that you have little strength, yet you have kept my word and have not denied my name"*, and also: *"Since you have kept my command to endure patiently..."* The book of Proverbs 20:6 says *"Many a man claims to have unfailing love, but a faithful man who can find?"* The Lord loves faithfulness, and He is seeking the remnant who stand for Him, who are faithful to His call, and who walk in His Word, no matter what. He is looking for a people who will tolerate no compromise, and who will allow His Word to seep into every aspect of their daily lives - not just their spirituality, but their finances, relationships, work and home. He is seeking a people who in these end times will represent the character and nature of Jesus on the earth - love, faithfulness, victory and overcoming. Surely we are a people of power!

This letter was written to the church of Philadelphia. Philadelphia was a city of Lydia in Asia Minor, about 25 miles south-east of Sardis. It came into the possession of the Turks in A.D. 1392. Many times it was nearly destroyed by earthquakes but survived to be a town of considerable size and importance. It is really significant that the word 'Philadelphia' means *brotherly love*! In these last days, God is calling us to be Philadelphians! More than anything else, God seeks that we walk in love towards our fellow men and women, especially those of the fellowship of faith. To survive these tough times, to experience God's blanket of protection, to emerge as a 'city of God', knowing His presence and power always, the Lord Jesus calls us to live in the same love we receive from the Father - forgiving, enduring, unconditional, unprejudiced love! It is to be our spiritual covering in these difficult times. (Colossians 3:14: *"And over all these virtues put on love, which binds them all together in perfect unity."*) It is our weapon of spiritual warfare! We speak God's language and raise up His banner when we walk in love.

As we cry out to the Holy Spirit to be our Help and Enabler, remember that Jesus said *'I am coming soon'!* The time is short. Our struggle will not be for much longer. He promised that once He returns, we will be with Him, worshipping Him forever - never to be separated from His awesome and glorious presence; and He will bring us into an intimate, heavenly revelation of the Father and the Son; the ultimate truths of the Kingdom - the new Jerusalem - His name will be branded upon us forever! May our hearts be opened to what the Holy Spirit is saying to the Bride of Christ. Let us hear what the Spirit says to the church.

I pray that God will see our hearts as faithful to His Word always. May we stand for His name and His Word against all odds. May we know His powerful protection in the hour of fiery trial, and walk in victory every day. Jesus is coming soon!

Notes:

Chapter Twenty Six

The Power In The Seed
(John 12:20-26)

"Now there were some Greeks among those who went up to worship at the Feast. They came to Philip, who was from Bethsaida in Galilee, with a request. "Sir," they said, "we would like to see Jesus." Philip went to tell Andrew; Andrew and Philip in turn told Jesus.

Jesus replied, "The hour has come for the Son of Man to be glorified. I tell you the truth, unless a grain of wheat falls to the ground and dies, it remains only a single seed. But if it dies, it produces many seeds. The man who loves his life will lose it, while the man who hates his life in this world will keep it for eternal life. Whoever serves me must follow me; and where I am, my servant also will be. My Father will honor the one who serves me."

It was a few days before the crucifixion of the Lord Jesus, and He was already in Jerusalem, when He was approached by some people who desired to meet Him. We are told that they were foreigners (Greeks), who had come to worship in Jerusalem, and celebrate the Passover. It is possible that they approached Philip because they already knew him, or because he spoke their language (the name 'Philip' is from the Greek name 'Philipos'); or because he was from the cosmo-politan coastal city of Bethsaida, which saw many foreign travelers passing through. They had heard about Jesus, and sought to meet Him. They were in Jerusalem to worship at the Feast, but their worship would only be complete if they met with Jesus!

Jesus said *"The hour has come for the Son of Man to be glorified."* Here were these people from another nation seeking after Jesus in Jerusalem because He is *"the desire of all nations"* - Haggai 2:7. Within a few days, the precious life of the Lamb of God would be sacrificed to bring redemption to all people from all nations and races of the world. When the Lord Jesus walked the road to Jerusalem and laid down His life in obedience to the will of God, it was the beginning of the fulfillment of God's great plan of salvation for all mankind. It was in humbling Himself to the will of the Father and laying down His life that the name of Jesus was truly glorified. He died to His own will and desires and God exalted and glorified Him forever. Jesus said in Matthew 23:12 *"For whoever exalts himself will be humbled, and whoever humbles himself will be exalted."*

When Jesus referred to the grain of wheat which had to fall to the ground and die, He was talking about His own life, which had to be laid down, and buried, for life and salvation to flow for the millions who have believed and received. He was the immortal Seed of God, who submitted to the laws of mortality, that the bounds of mortality be broken and the gift of eternal life made available to all who sought Him. He 'fell to the ground' when He descended from Heaven to earth, and when He stepped from earth to death upon the cross. From that Seed that died, life burst forth for the countless souls that received Him and became sons and daughters of the Most High. God sowed the Seed of His Son, and from the 'death' of that Seed came an uncountable family!

There is a message of freedom, power and increase in what Jesus said to His disciples. He said *"The man who loves his life will lose it, while the man who hates his life in this world will keep it eternally..."* When we let go of what is most precious to us, and release it to God, He blesses it, and gives it back to us multiplied and overflowing! This can apply to everything in our lives. It applies to what is most dear to your heart, perhaps the source of your greatest joy, as well as the cause of your deepest pain. It could be your career ambitions or your child; it could be your spouse or your ministry. It is the passion of your heart, and whatever that passion may be, the Lord Jesus is asking you today to lay it at His feet. Let it "fall to the ground". Stop striving to "make it happen." As you release it to Jesus, you will see it blessed and increased to abundance. As you lay your own plans down 'on the ground' you will see better ones brought forth by the Father, as He opens doors that no man could have opened. For example, if you have been praying for God's provision in your finances, the way to see your harvest is to start sowing in faith into fertile Kingdom ground. As that seed falls to the ground, and your every desire and anxiety for it is allowed to die, it will begin to take root within the earth, and life, power and harvest will burst out of it and into your hand. It is a spiritual principle that can never fail. God's Word can never return void.

These words of Jesus also help us to look at what our lives are really based on, and what we love the most; whether they are things of eternal value or the things of the world which are for today and gone tomorrow. He said in Matthew 6:21: *"Where your treasure is, there your heart will be also"*. Our physical existence is to be enjoyed and blessed, but is it lived to the exclusion of those eternal and spiritual things which God has called us to walk in? Are we investing in treasures of an eternal nature, or is our life and passion knitted solely into our earthly existence? Jesus said to His disciples that if what is physical and worldly was all they were focused on, they would lose the other life which was for eternity, and God's gift to be received in faith.

Everything in the Kingdom is based on the seed falling to the ground. There is no return without the investment of the seed. Galatians 6:7-9 say *"A man reaps what he sows. The one who sows to please his sinful nature, from that nature will reap destruc-*

tion; the one who sows to please the Spirit will reap eternal life. Let us not become weary in doing good, for at the proper time we will reap a harvest, if we do not give up." Serving Jesus means following Him – living as He lived, loving as He loved, and giving as He gave, even His own life! And He promises that when we serve Him and walk as He walked, we will be "where He is"; on another level of love, faith and power, with signs and wonders following us, and victory over every challenge and attack of the enemy. It means 'carrying' Heaven with us wherever we go, because God promises to honor those who are faithful to Jesus! His presence goes with us, and He surrounds us with His favor, as with a shield (Psalm 5: 12).

And finally, we always tend to reject the thought of something (or someone) dying or coming to an end, but there is always something greater that comes from a seed that dies. When Jesus died upon that cruel cross, his disciples mourned Him, and wept for what they thought were shattered dreams; but from His death on the cross came resurrection and life, and power over sin, sickness and death for all humanity. In the same way, the earthly 'end' of a child of God only means more beautiful resurrected life in the presence of the Father for eternity; it is the beginning of the rest of the story! New life always springs forth from what is laid to rest. The death of the seed brings life in the form of new plants that spring up through the ground. Winter has to give way to spring! There is abundance and blessing to come, but first the seed has to die in the womb of the earth, just as your own dreams have to be laid to rest, but only to receive the greater ones which God has for you.

We can take some threads of Truth from what Jesus said to His disciples. He is calling us to:

1) **Seek God's will and flow with it.** This is what He did when He laid His life down in fulfillment of the Father's plan for the salvation of man. He is calling us to lay down our own will, die to our own plans and desires, and surrender to what God wants to do through our lives. This is the path to power!

2) **Lay down what you have been struggling to keep or achieve. Give what you want to receive.** Jesus sowed His life for the salvation of every man, woman and child doomed to eternal death. He said in John 10:17-18 *"The reason my Father loves Me is that I lay down My life – only to take it up again. No one takes it from Me, but I lay it down of My own accord."* Whatever you have been praying for and want to receive, sow into the life or ministry of another.

3) **Follow the Master and obey God** – you will see the Father honor you as you walk in His favor, and the presence of Jesus will be your daily portion. (Proverbs 27:18 says *"He who looks after his master will be honored"*). You will walk in the anointing and power of Jesus as you walk in His will!

4) **There is power in the seed** – but it has to be laid to rest.

May you see great blessing and fruitful harvest in every area of your life, as you lay it down at the feet of Jesus and allow the seed to die. You are giving way to something better and bigger. There is power in the seed that falls!

Notes:

Chapter Twenty Seven

Breakthrough
(Luke 13:10-13)

"On a Sabbath Jesus was teaching in one of the synagogues, and a woman was there who had been crippled by a spirit for eighteen years. She was bent over and could not straighten up at all. When Jesus saw her, he called her forward and said to her, "Woman, you are set free from your infirmity." Then He put His hands on her, and immediately she straightened up and praised God."

This is a message about breakthrough! It is for the many precious people of God who have been crying out to God day after day, and praying for a radical change in their lives.

This passage of Scripture talks about a woman who knew and worshipped God - she was in the synagogue when Jesus met her; but we see that for eighteen long years she had been bound by a crippling spirit which had stopped her enjoying a normal life. She had been bent over, unable to run or dance, or lift up her hands to the skies and sing songs of praise to the Lord. She had been unable to appreciate the beauty of a sunset, or the smiles on the faces of the ones she loved. What she usually saw was the hard ground and the dust of the road, because her back was bent over and her face was down. It is possible that she also experienced pain and discomfort. Normal aspects of life which we take for granted - like dressing or climbing steps must have been difficult and even painful for her. Her household chores, (like drawing water from a well), must have been agony. Imagine suffering this way for 18 years! She was living at less than the level God had for her. She probably came to the synagogue week after week and listened to the reading of the Scriptures. Maybe she wondered if they were true, and if God was real. Perhaps she wondered if He knew of her existence, and whether there was a chance that God could reach out and touch her twisted body. She may have lived in hope at the start, but it is likely that her problem got progressively worse. As the years came and went, it could be that her disability was so much a part of her identity that she could not really think of a life in which she could be whole and normal – her mind and heart became as bent over as her back, as the years passed and her faith shrank.

Jesus says in John 10:10 that He came that we may have life, and have it to the full! God's will is that every aspect of our lives be immersed in His blessing, but the thief steals, kills and destroys the fullness of life which is ours; he seeks to make us walk under the curse when Jesus has already made all provision for us to walk in the blessing.

This dear lady, (whom Jesus referred to as a 'daughter of Abraham') was probably just clocking in her weekly visit to the synagogue the day she received her breakthrough; but **she was in the right place at the right time!** The Lord Jesus, the Healer and Restorer of souls and bodies walked into the church that day. When His presence came into the service, things began to happen. Blind eyes were opened and deaf ears began to hear. The anointing and the power of the blessed Holy Spirit flowed as people who had been bound for years were set free! This lady knew someone special was in the room because she could feel the difference in the atmosphere. She knew things were happening and heard the shouts of joy and praise as people were healed! As she turned her neck sideways, she could probably see the feet of people running towards the Lord, jumping and rejoicing. But because her eyes were mostly focused on the floor, she could not really see the compassionate eyes of the Master or His healing hands.

Then the eyes of Jesus fell on her! She heard Him call her forward, and as the people pushed her along to the front of the synagogue, she felt her heart fill with hope. The radiant waves of power got stronger as she got closer. And as she got to Him, she could barely stay still before him because of the awesome anointing He emanated – she felt dizzy and light! Her moment had come. She believed! She heard the words that changed her life - *"Woman, you are set free from your infirmity"!* Jesus saw her for who she was – *a woman* – needy, frail, weighed down by her problem. A woman whose heart had once been full of dreams, hopes and secret ambitions, whose life had once been filled with laughter and joy. He saw her in all her frustration and pain, and the rejection and isolation of her infirm life. For many years she had lived on the fringes of society, unable to do many things other women could. He saw her disappointments and broken dreams. She was so bent over with the burden she carried, that she could not see the smile upon His face. For eighteen years she had lived with a pain which went deeper than the physical. It was an oppression, a bondage that had held her captive, repressed and unable to know the abundant life which was hers to have. As the words of Jesus settled upon her and penetrated into the depths of her soul to explode out in faith for healing, Jesus laid His hands on her, and she was immediately healed! A crippling infirmity of 18 years was healed in an instant!

The precious Holy Spirit reminds me as these words flow that there are many daughters and sons of Abraham, who have suffered months and years with infirmity, turbulent marriages and family problems. Others are battling financial lack, fears, addictions and compulsive habits which they want freedom from. Many of us are bent over with the weight of the burden we carry. Satan has brought crippling difficulties and bondage to stop the people of God from enjoying the fullness of the blessing Jesus died to make possible. They have been robbed of the joy and peace, and the power for victory which is their portion. They have lost the freedom which Jesus paid a high price for! The weight of the burden they carry has made it difficult to look upwards at the sunshine of God's love, or see the heights to which the Holy Spirit can take them. They are unable to lift up their eyes to the hills from where their help comes (Psalm 121). The mundane, ground-level issues and the complexity of their problems have totally absorbed their attention.

The Lord Jesus recognized the source and cause of the deformity of this dear lady's back. In Luke 13:16, He said to His critics *"...should not this woman, a daughter of Abraham, whom Satan has kept bound for eighteen long years, be set free on the Sabbath day from what bound her?"* Many people of God do not see or deal with the true root of their difficulties, as the work of Satan in their lives. Paul wrote to the Ephesian church (Ephesians 6:12) *"For our struggle is not against flesh and blood, but against the rulers, against the authorities, against the powers of this dark world and against the spiritual forces of evil in the heavenly realms."* Modern science has made great advances in the field of medicine, and there are medicines that can alleviate physical symptoms to a great degree. However, instead of depending on prolonged medication and other seeming solutions the world offers, we need to address the root cause – the spiritual forces of darkness – and not stop with the symptoms. **Breakthrough begins when we recognize the source of our problem and begin to deal with it.** We can start by asking our Father to show us the root causes of the problems we face and allow Him to guide us in the steps we take.

Notice that the crippled woman began to receive her healing when she heard and received the powerful, living Words of Jesus into her life and upon her body. Something began to happen when she heard Him call her and she obeyed. When she came into His presence, and He laid His hands upon her she was totally healed! She had been coming to church each week for many years, but never experienced a healing until she encountered the presence of Jesus. When His glory touched her, her chains were broken. Her twisted spinal chord and crooked bones and muscles were miraculously made straight. She could feel her body vibrating with the power of the Holy Spirit as bones, nerves, muscles and flesh were all corrected and made whole! Her life was transformed. For the first time in eighteen years she stood up straight and her mouth was filled with praises unto God! What joy and gratitude must have filled her heart. I believe she jumped and skipped, and danced all the way home! John 8:36 says *"...if the Son sets you free, you will be free indeed."*

Precious child of God, the Holy Spirit is speaking to you today and imparting a blessing upon you as you read this message. Draw near to the Lord and worship Him! Begin to receive the Words of Jesus upon your body and your mind. Absorb them into your spirit. As the servant of the living God, I say to you today in the power of the Holy Spirit and in the name of Jesus Christ that **God has set you free!** Whatever the situation that has crippled you and held you on a level less than what God wished for you, **be loosed** today, in Jesus' name! For those in need, may every spirit of lack be broken off your life and family, and may you know the overflowing and abundant provision of the Father. For those who need a healing touch, may every spirit of infirmity and pain be broken off every part of your body and mind, and may you and your family know a healing and wholeness you never knew before. For anyone bound by addictions, may the spirits that have tormented your mind and held you captive to addictions or compulsions in thought and deed be broken from your life. I apply the blood of Jesus Christ the Savior and Healer upon your mind and body today.

Whatever the burden you have been carrying, **be healed, be free, be restored, be blessed in Jesus' name!** Expect great transformations because that is what God wills for you! May the presence and power of God's Holy Spirit be your portion!

Notes:

References

Bible History - www.bible-history.com

Bible Places Encyclopedia - www.bibleplaces.com

Easton's Bible Dictionary - www.eastonsbibledictio nary.com

Holman Bible Dictionary - www.studylight.org.dic. hbd

Hitchcock's Bible Dictionary - www.searchgodsword. org/dic/hbn

Jewish Life Cycles - www.templesanjose.org

Matthew Henry's Commentary, (Edited by Leslie F Church, PhD), Zondervan Press, Grand Rapids, Michigan, USA.

NIV Study Bible, Zondervan Corporation, Michigan, 1985

ScriptureTextMultilingual Bible - www.scripturetext. com

Teachings of Perry Stone on Jewish Marriage Rites

Wikipedia On-Line Encyclopedia - wikipedia.org/wiki

The author can be contacted through the website

www.wingslikeeagles.info

Breinigsville, PA USA
15 September 2010
245456BV00001B/1/P